The Delia Collection
Chicken

BBC
BOOKS

Published by BBC Books
BBC Worldwide Ltd
Woodlands
80 Wood Lane
London W12 OTT

First published in 2003

Edited for BBC Worldwide Ltd
by New Crane Ltd

Editor: Sarah Randell
Designer: Paul Webster
Sub-editor: Heather Cupit
Picture Editor: Diana Hughes
Recipe Testing: Pauline Curran
Commissioning Editor for the BBC: Vivien Bowler

ISBN 0 563 48731 3

Printed and bound in Singapore
by Tien Wah Press Ltd
Colour separation by Radstock Reproductions Ltd
Midsomer Norton

Cover and title-page photographs: Michael Paul
For further photographic credits, see page 136

Introduction

When I look back over my years of cookery writing, I have to admit that very often, decisions about what to do have sprung from what my own particular needs are. As a very busy person, who has to work, run a home and cook, I felt it was extremely useful to have, for instance, summer recipes in one book – likewise winter and Christmas, giving easy access to those specific seasons.

This, my latest venture, has come about for similar reasons. Thirty three years of recipe writing have produced literally thousands of recipes. So I now feel what would be really helpful is to create a kind of ordered library (so I don't have to rack my brains and wonder which book this or that recipe is in!). Thus, if I want to make a chicken recipe, I don't have to look through the chicken sections of various books, but have the whole lot in one convenient collection.

In compiling these collections, I have chosen what I think are the best and most popular recipes and, at the same time, have added some that are completely new. It is my hope that those who have not previously tried my recipes will now have smaller collections to sample, and that those dedicated followers will appreciate an ordered library to provide easy access and a reminder of what has gone before and may have been forgotten.

Delia Smith

Conversion Tables

All these are approximate conversions, which have either been rounded up or down. In a few recipes it has been necessary to modify them very slightly. Never mix metric and imperial measures in one recipe, stick to one system or the other.

All spoon measurements used throughout this book are level unless specified otherwise.

All butter is salted unless specified otherwise.

All recipes have been double-tested, using a standard convection oven. If you are using a fan oven, adjust the cooking temperature according to the manufacturer's handbook.

Weights

½ oz	10 g
¾	20
1	25
1½	40
2	50
2½	60
3	75
4	110
4½	125
5	150
6	175
7	200
8	225
9	250
10	275
12	350
1 lb	450
1 lb 8 oz	700
2	900
3	1.35 kg

Volume

2 fl oz	55 ml
3	75
5 (¼ pint)	150
10 (½ pint)	275
1 pint	570
1¼	725
1¾	1 litre
2	1.2
2½	1.5
4	2.25

Dimensions

⅛ inch	3 mm
¼	5
½	1 cm
¾	2
1	2.5
1¼	3
1½	4
1¾	4.5
2	5
2½	6
3	7.5
3½	9
4	10
5	13
5¼	13.5
6	15
6½	16
7	18
7½	19
8	20
9	23
9½	24
10	25.5
11	28
12	30

Oven temperatures

Gas mark 1	275°F	140°C
2	300	150
3	325	170
4	350	180
5	375	190
6	400	200
7	425	220
8	450	230
9	475	240

Contents

Spring page 7
Summer page 37
Autumn page 69
Winter page 97

Traditional Gravy and Other Sauces page 127
How to Carve a Chicken page 131
Index page 134

Spring

Fast-roast Chicken
with Lemon and Tarragon
Serves 4

a 3 lb (1.35 kg) chicken

1 small lemon: ½ of it thinly sliced and the slices halved, plus the juice of the remaining ½ lemon

2½ tablespoons chopped fresh tarragon leaves

2 cloves garlic, crushed

½ oz (10 g) softened butter

1 dessertspoon olive oil

10 fl oz (275 ml) dry white wine

salt and freshly milled black pepper

You will also need a solid-based, flameproof roasting tin, 9 x 11 inches (23 x 28 cm), and 2 inches (5 cm) deep.

Pre-heat the oven to gas mark 8, 450°F (230°C).

This is the best way to roast a small chicken. The flavourings can vary in any way you like – crushed chopped rosemary leaves, sage leaves or thyme can be used, or a mixture of herbs, and you could replace the garlic with a couple of finely chopped shallots. It's a great recipe for adapting to whatever you have handy.

Begin by taking the chicken from the fridge about an hour before you intend to cook it (if it's a hot day give it about 30 minutes only), and remove the string that holds the legs of the bird together so that the joints are loose – this will take the chill off the bird and help it to cook in the shorter time.

Now make a garlic and herb butter by placing the garlic, 2 tablespoons of the chopped tarragon leaves and the butter in a bowl and combine them with a fork, adding some salt and pepper. Then place the herb butter inside the body cavity of the bird, along with the halved lemon slices. Smear a little of the olive oil over the base of the roasting tin, place the chicken in it, then smear the rest of the olive oil all over the skin of the bird. Lastly, season well with salt and black pepper and then pop the roasting tin into the lower third of the oven. Now let it roast for 45 minutes without opening the oven door. When this time is up, remove the bird from the oven. Next, put a wooden spoon into the body cavity and, using a spatula to hold the breast end, tip the chicken and let all the buttery juices and slices of lemon pour out into the roasting tin, then transfer the bird on to a carving board, cover with foil and let it rest for 20 minutes.

Meanwhile, using a tablespoon, skim off the excess fat from the juices in the roasting tin, then place the tin over direct heat, add the wine and lemon juice and let the whole lot bubble and reduce to about half its original volume. Now add the remaining tarragon, then taste and check the seasoning. Carve the chicken and place on to warm plates and add any juices to the sauce. Spoon the sauce over the chicken and serve.

Oriental Chicken
Serves 2

4 plump chicken thighs

5 fl oz (150 ml) Shaosing
(Chinese brown rice wine)

3 fl oz (75 ml) Japanese soy sauce

1 heaped teaspoon grated
fresh root ginger

4 cloves garlic, crushed

5 whole star anise

1 teaspoon toasted sesame oil

To garnish

1 small red chilli, deseeded and
cut into fine shreds

1 spring onion, cut into fine shreds
(including the green parts)

You will also need a small,
flameproof casserole.

Pre-heat the oven to gas mark 6,
400°F (200°C).

It's hard to believe something so easy can firstly, be low fat and secondly, taste so very good. I guarantee that once you've made this once, you'll go on making it for ever.

First of all, remove the skin from the chicken, then place the chicken thighs in the casserole. Now mix the rest of the ingredients together in a bowl with 2 fl oz (55 ml) water and pour this mixture over the chicken, place the casserole over a medium heat and bring the liquid to the boil.

Now transfer it to the oven (no need to cover) and bake on the centre shelf for 40 minutes, turning the chicken halfway through the cooking time. Serve the cooked chicken on a bed of plain rice with the sauce poured over and the shreds of chilli and spring onion sprinkled on top.

Grilled Chicken with Lemon, Garlic and Rosemary, served with Puy Lentils
Serves 2

2 boneless chicken breasts
(6 oz/175 g) each, skin on

grated zest of 1 lemon, plus
3 tablespoons of fresh lemon juice

1 clove garlic, crushed

1 tablespoon fresh rosemary
leaves, bruised and finely chopped

1 medium red onion, halved

2 bay leaves, snipped in half

3 tablespoons extra virgin olive oil

4 small open-cap mushrooms

salt and freshly milled
black pepper

For the lentils

5 oz (150 g) Puy lentils

½ red onion (see above)

1 dessertspoon extra virgin
olive oil

8 fl oz (225 ml) red or white wine
or water

a fresh rosemary sprig

salt and freshly milled
black pepper

To garnish

fresh flat-leaf parsley

You will also need two wooden
bamboo skewers, 10 inches
(25.5 cm) long. Alternatively,
use metal skewers.

This recipe is for the stressed, overworked man or woman who still wants to eat real food when they finally get home. All you do is shove the chicken in the marinade, go off to have a nice relaxing shower, followed by something that includes the sound of ice tinkling on glass, and then, when you're finally ready for supper, it will only take about 40 minutes. On the other hand, if you have time, marinate it for longer – or even the night before.

Begin by cutting each chicken breast into 5 evenly sized pieces and place these in a bowl. Then cut one half of the onion into quarters and separate into layers, adding them to the chicken, along with the rest of the ingredients and a seasoning of salt and pepper. Now give everything a good mixing, cover with a cloth and go away and leave it in a cool place for at least half an hour.

While you are marinating the chicken, if you are using wooden skewers you need to soak them for 30 minutes in hot water (to prevent them burning). Then when you're ready to cook the chicken, pre-heat the grill for 10 minutes to its highest setting and set the grill tray 4 inches (10 cm) from the element. Next, see to the lentils. Just chop the other half of the onion finely, heat the oil in a medium saucepan, fry the onion for about 5 minutes, then stir in the lentils, making sure they get a good coating of oil. Then add the liquid and sprig of rosemary. Put on a lid and let the lentils simmer gently for about 30-40 minutes until the liquid has been absorbed.

To cook the chicken, thread the pieces on the skewers, putting half a bay leaf first, then a mushroom, next a piece of chicken, then a piece of onion, finishing with the other mushroom and the other half of the bay leaf. Then, keeping the skin side of the chicken pieces upwards, lay the skewers on the grill rack, with a dish underneath to catch the juices. Season them well, then grill for 20 minutes, turning once and basting with the marinade juices once or twice. When the chicken is ready, taste and season the lentils with salt and a little freshly milled black pepper and arrange them on warm serving plates. Slide the chicken, onion and bay leaf off the skewers between the prongs of a fork, then spoon the warm basting juices over everything. Garnish with flat-leaf parsley and serve with the lentils and a green salad.

Stir-fried Chicken with Lime and Coconut
Serves 2

2 boneless, skinless
chicken breasts

grated zest and juice of
1 large lime

5 fl oz (150 ml) tinned
coconut milk

1 dessertspoon olive oil

1 green chilli, deseeded
and finely chopped

1 dessertspoon Thai fish sauce

4 heaped tablespoons fresh
coriander leaves

4 spring onions, cut into
1 inch (2.5 cm) shreds
(including the green parts),
to garnish

You will also need a frying pan
with a diameter of 10 inches
(25.5 cm), or a wok.

It's hard to credit that a recipe as simple and as quick as this could taste so good, but I can assure you it's an absolute winner and makes a very speedy supper dish for two.

First of all, chop the chicken into bite-sized pieces and place them in a bowl with the lime juice and zest. Stir well, cover and leave them to marinate in a cool place for an hour.

When you're ready to cook the chicken, heat the oil in the pan or wok over a high heat, add the chicken pieces and stir-fry for 3-4 minutes, until they're golden. Then add the chilli, stir-fry for 1 more minute, and add the coconut milk, fish sauce and half the coriander and spring onions. Cook for another 1-2 minutes, then serve with the remaining coriander and the spring onions sprinkled over. Serve with Thai fragrant rice.

Mexican Chicken Chilli with Yellow Tomato Salsa
Serves 6

2 lb 4 oz (1 kg) skinless, boneless chicken thighs

6 medium green chillies, deseeded and finely chopped

1 oz (25 g) fresh coriander

2 tablespoons olive oil

2 large onions, sliced

4 cloves garlic, crushed

1 heaped teaspoon cumin seeds

9 oz (250 g) pinto beans, soaked overnight and drained

1 tablespoon plain flour

1 pint (570 ml) hot chicken stock

1 teaspoon Tabasco sauce

1 large green pepper

8 oz (225 g) mozzarella, grated

2½ fl oz (65 ml) double cream

juice of ½ lime

salt and freshly milled black pepper

For the salsa

9 oz (250 g) yellow or red tomatoes

half the reserved coriander leaves, roughly chopped

½ small red onion, finely chopped

juice of ½ lime

a few drops of Tabasco sauce

salt and freshly milled black pepper

You will also need a lidded, flameproof casserole with a capacity of 6 pints (3.5 litres).

I have to admit they probably won't have heard of this in Mexico, but I've so named it because it's a dish based on a couple of Mexican themes: firstly, there are the delightful pinto beans, and secondly, the cheese is melted into the sauce. Anyway, Mexican or not, it's a great recipe. You should, ideally, start this the day before to soak the beans, but if you haven't the time for this, simply cover them with water, bring to the boil, boil for 10 minutes and leave them to soak for two hours before draining.

Begin by stripping the coriander leaves into a small bowl, then cover it with clingfilm and pop it into the fridge. Now chop the coriander stalks very finely. Next, heat the oil in the casserole and, over a gentle heat, cook the onions, garlic, chillies and coriander stalks for about 10 minutes, stirring once or twice until softened.

Meanwhile, dry-roast the cumin seeds in a frying pan for about a minute or until they become fragrant. Then grind the seeds to a powder in a pestle and mortar, then add them, along with the drained beans, to the casserole and stir. Now sprinkle in the flour and give it another good stir. Next, gradually add the stock, followed by the Tabasco sauce and a little salt, bring everything to a simmer and cook, covered, on the lowest heat possible for 1¼-1½ hours, until the beans are tender.

In the meantime, make the salsa. First, skin, deseed and finely chop the tomatoes. Then simply combine half the reserved coriander leaves and the rest of the salsa ingredients and season. Mix well, then cover and leave aside to allow the flavours to develop.

When the chilli has had its initial cooking time, deseed the green pepper and cut it into ½ inch (1 cm) pieces. Now cut the chicken into bite-sized chunks and stir them, along with the pepper, into the casserole, season well with salt and freshly milled black pepper, cover, and simmer for a further 30 minutes.

In the meantime, mix the mozzarella with the double cream, then, when the 30 minutes are up, add it to the casserole. Simmer gently, uncovered, for a further 20-25 minutes, stirring now and again, by which time the cheese should have melted and formed a smooth sauce. Finally, stir in the lime juice and the remaining coriander leaves. Serve with a little rice and a green vegetable and hand the salsa round separately.

Poached Chicken Breasts with Morel Mushrooms, Cream and Parsley
Serves 4

4 chicken breasts

½ oz (10 g) dried morel or chanterelle mushrooms

4 tablespoons double cream

2 tablespoons finely chopped fresh parsley

1 pint (570 ml) dry white wine

4 oz (110 g) small, dark-gilled mushrooms, thinly sliced

4 large egg yolks

salt and freshly milled black pepper

This is lovely made with dried morel or chanterelle mushrooms and has a wonderful, light, creamy sauce! Dried porcini (cep) are also excellent but you will need to roughly chop them after soaking.

Start by soaking the morels or chanterelles. Place them in a small bowl, cover with boiling water and leave them aside to soak for 30 minutes. After that, strain them in a sieve and squeeze them to get rid of any surplus water. (You can reserve the soaking water, which can be frozen and is great for soups.)

Now pre-heat the oven to a low setting, ready to keep the chicken warm later. Next, in a large saucepan bring the wine up to simmering point, then add the chicken breasts, together with some salt and freshly milled pepper. Bring back up to simmering point, put a lid on, and simmer gently for 15 minutes. Then remove the chicken and keep it warm, covered, in a low oven.

Now boil the cooking liquid quite fast (without a lid) until it has reduced in volume by about a half, adding the fresh and dried mushrooms towards the end of this time, then remove the pan from the heat. Next, in a small basin, beat together the egg yolks and cream, and mix a couple of tablespoons of the hot cooking liquid into the egg mixture, then pour the whole mixture back in to join the rest in the saucepan.

Return the pan to a low heat and, stirring all the time, re-heat it until it thickens. Don't, whatever you do, let it come to the boil or it will separate! As soon as it has thickened, stir in the parsley and pour the mushroom sauce over the chicken and serve with roasted butternut squash.

Marinated Chicken Brochettes with Green Couscous
Serves 2

2 boneless chicken breasts
(6 oz/175 g each), skin removed

6 fresh bay leaves, cut in half

½ medium red onion, halved and
separated into 8 layers

½ large yellow pepper, deseeded
and cut into 8

1 teaspoon groundnut or other
flavourless oil

salt and freshly milled
black pepper

For the marinade

1 clove garlic

1 teaspoon grated fresh
root ginger

1 medium green chilli,
deseeded

1 tablespoon fresh coriander
leaves

1 teaspoon ground turmeric

6 fl oz (175 ml) buttermilk

salt and freshly milled
black pepper

For the couscous

5 oz (150 g) couscous

9 fl oz (250 ml) boiling chicken
or vegetable stock

4 spring onions
(including the green parts),
finely chopped

2 tablespoons chopped
fresh coriander

1 oz (25 g) rocket leaves,
finely chopped

This is a five-star recipe if you're watching your waistline because buttermilk makes a superb marinade – so much so you'll wonder why you ever needed oil. The chicken will be luscious and tender and, with all the other wonderful flavours, you won't notice this is a low-fat recipe. This is also good served with the Coriander Chutney (see page 62) – just halve the quantity.

First of all, you need to make the marinade. To do this, use a pestle and mortar to crush the garlic with about ½ teaspoon of salt until it becomes a purée. Next, add the grated fresh ginger. Then chop the chilli and coriander leaves and mix these with the garlic and ginger, along with the turmeric and some freshly milled black pepper. After that, pour the buttermilk into a bowl and whisk the other ingredients into it.

Now cut each chicken breast into 5 pieces, add them to the bowl and give everything a good stir. Then press the chicken down well into the marinade, cover the surface with clingfilm and pop the bowl into the fridge for a few hours or, preferably, overnight. When you are almost ready to cook the chicken, if using wooden skewers, soak them in hot water for 30 minutes (to prevent them burning). Pre-heat the grill to its highest setting for at least 10 minutes and line the grill pan with kitchen foil.

Next, dry the skewers in a clean tea cloth and thread half a bay leaf on to each one, then a piece of chicken, a piece of onion and a piece of pepper. Carry on alternating the bay leaf, chicken, onion and pepper until you have threaded 5 pieces of chicken on to each skewer, finishing with half a bay leaf on each. Make sure you pack everything together as tightly as possible, then season with salt and freshly milled black pepper and brush the vegetables with a minute amount of oil. Lay the brochettes on the grill rack and place them under the grill, about 4 inches (10 cm) from the heat source. Brush liberally with some of the remaining marinade and grill them for 10 minutes, before turning them over and grilling them for a further 10 minutes, brushing them with more of the marinade as they cook, and watching them carefully so they don't burn.

While the chicken is cooking, place the couscous in a largish bowl, then pour the boiling stock over it, add some salt and freshly milled black pepper and stir it with

1 lime cut into wedges, to serve

salt and freshly milled
black pepper

You will also need two wooden
skewers, 10 inches (25.5 cm) long.
Alternatively, use metal skewers.

a fork. Then leave it on one side for 5 minutes, by which time it will have absorbed all the stock and softened. After that, fluff it up by making cutting movements across and through it with a knife. Then stir in the remaining couscous ingredients and season to taste. When the chicken is ready, pop the brochettes on top of the couscous and serve straightaway on warmed serving plates, served with the wedges of lime.

Creamed Chicken with Avocado
Serves 4

a 1 lb (450 g) cold, cooked chicken, cut into small strips

2 ripe avocados

2 oz (50 g) butter

2 oz (50 g) plain flour

10 fl oz (275 ml) milk

5 fl oz (150 ml) chicken stock

5 fl oz (150 ml) single cream

1 tablespoon dry sherry

2-3 teaspoons lemon juice

1 oz (25 g) Gruyère, grated

salt and freshly milled black pepper

You will also need an 8 inch (20 cm) square, ovenproof baking dish, 2 inches (5 cm) deep.

Pre-heat the oven to gas mark 6, 400°F (200°C).

This is one for someone in a hurry, as it's made with ready-cooked chicken, which is now widely available in supermarkets. But don't be put off – it ends up tasting very classy.

Begin by melting the butter in a medium saucepan, add the flour and blend to a smooth paste. Cook for 2 minutes, then gradually stir in the milk, stock and cream and, stirring all the time, bring it to simmering point and cook very gently for 2 or 3 minutes. Then remove the pan from the heat, add the chicken pieces, sherry, salt, pepper and lemon juice to taste and stir everything together until combined.

Now halve and quarter the avocados and, having removed the stone and skins, slice the flesh thinly and cover the base of the dish with the slices. Sprinkle over a little lemon juice, spoon the chicken mixture on top and, finally, add the grated cheese. Transfer to the pre-heated oven and bake from 20-25 minutes or until the sides start to bubble.

Marinated Chicken in a Jar
Serves 2

2 boneless chicken breasts
(about 6 oz/175 g each), skin on

½ red onion

½ yellow pepper, deseeded

½ tablespoon chopped fresh
thyme leaves

½ tablespoon chopped fresh
rosemary

2 bay leaves

2 slices of lemon, cut in half

10 whole black peppercorns

2 cloves garlic

2 fl oz (55 ml) white wine vinegar
or cider vinegar

4 fl oz (120 ml) extra virgin olive oil

salt and freshly milled
black pepper

You will also need a 17½ fl oz
(500 ml) jar, plus two bamboo
skewers, 8 inches (20 cm)
long. Alternatively, use metal
skewers.

This is utterly simple, but it does need a little planning as the chicken benefits from 24 hours in the marinade in the jar. Try to start the marinade off the night before, and then if you are out at work all day, you can come home to the fastest supper on earth, as all you then do is thread the ingredients on to skewers and pop them under the grill.

Begin by cutting each chicken breast into 5 pieces and placing them in the jar. Then cut the onion into 2 quarters and separate the layers (you'll need 8). Now cut the deseeded pepper into 8 pieces and add these to the jar, along with the chopped herbs, bay leaves, lemon and peppercorns. Now crush a clove of garlic and add this, too, plus the other clove, cut in half. Next, pour in the vinegar, followed by the oil, put the lid on the jar and give it a really good shake. Leave it in the fridge overnight and give it another good shake in the morning before you go out.

Before cooking the chicken, if you are using wooden skewers you need to soak them for 30 minutes in hot water (to prevent them burning), then pre-heat the grill to its highest setting for 10 minutes. Then thread a bay leaf on to each skewer, followed by a slice of lemon. Then alternate the chicken pieces with pepper and onion, finishing up with half a clove of garlic and the other slice of lemon. Add a seasoning of salt and pepper, then lay the skewers on a grill rack, skin side up, with a dish below to catch the juices. Position them about 4 inches (10 cm) from the source of the heat, then grill – turning once and brushing frequently with the marinade – for 20 minutes. These are very nice served with rice and a mixed lettuce and rocket salad.

Chicken Paprika
Serves 4

4 part-boned chicken breasts or 8 thighs

1 heaped tablespoon hot paprika, plus a little extra, to sprinkle

2-3 tablespoons groundnut or other flavourless oil

2 medium onions, chopped

1 dessertspoon plain flour

2 good pinches of cayenne pepper

1 lb (450 g) ripe tomatoes, skinned and chopped or 14 oz (400 g) tinned Italian tomatoes

5 fl oz (150 ml) chicken stock

1 medium green or red pepper, deseeded and cut into small strips

5 fl oz (150 ml) soured cream

salt and freshly milled black pepper

You will also need a 6 pint (3.5 litre), lidded, deep frying pan or casserole.

Pre-heat the oven to gas mark 3, 325°F (170°C).

This is nice served with some well buttered noodles or some nutty brown basmati rice and a crisp green salad with a sharp, lemony dressing, or instead, serve with green tagliatelle tossed in butter with a sprinkle of poppy seeds.

Begin by heating 2 tablespoons of the oil in the frying pan or casserole and gently frying the chicken joints or thighs to a golden colour, you will probably need to do this in two batches. As the chicken is ready, use a draining spoon to transfer it to a plate, and season it with salt and pepper. In the oil left (add a little more if you need to) fry the onions gently for about 10 minutes to soften. Meanwhile, if you are using fresh tomatoes, you can skin them. To do this, pour boiling water over them and leave them for exactly 1 minute or 15-30 seconds if the tomatoes are small, before draining and slipping off their skins (protect your hands with a cloth if they are too hot). Then chop them.

Now stir the flour, cayenne and paprika into the onions, with a wooden spoon, to soak up the juices before adding the chopped tomatoes. Stir them around a bit, then add the stock. Bring everything up to a simmering point, then return the chicken to the pan or casserole, put the lid on and bake in the oven for 45 minutes. After that, stir in the chopped pepper, replace the lid and cook for a further 30 minutes.

Just before serving, spoon the soured cream all over, mixing it in just to give a marbled effect, then sprinkle on a little more paprika.

Spanish Chicken with Butter Beans, Chorizo and Tomatoes
Serves 4

4 part-boned chicken breasts, skin on

8 oz (225 g) dried butter beans or judion beans, soaked overnight and drained

2 tablespoons olive oil

6 oz (175 g) chorizo sausage (raw chorizo, if available, is best for this)

14 oz (400 g) tin chopped plum tomatoes

a few sprigs of fresh thyme

2 bay leaves

1 medium onion

2 medium carrots

1 medium leek

2 sticks celery

1 teaspoon sweet pimentón (smoked paprika)

3 cloves garlic, chopped

a good pinch of saffron stamens

10 fl oz (275 ml) hot vegetable or chicken stock

2 tablespoons chopped fresh parsley

salt and freshly milled black pepper

You will also need a 6 pint (3.5 litre), lidded, flameproof casserole.

This recipe comes from our Executive Chef, Lucy Crabb, at the football club, and it's been served both at large banquets and in the restaurant to great acclaim. A rocket and chicory salad is a good accompaniment.

First of all, begin by cooking the butter beans. Place the soaked and drained beans in a pan with the sprigs of thyme and 1 of the bay leaves and cover with water. Bring to simmering point and then cover with a lid and simmer the beans for 45 minutes to 1 hour or until the beans are tender. Meanwhile, prepare the vegetables. Begin by peeling the onion and carrots and finely chopping them. Next, take the tough green ends off the leek, then make a vertical split halfway down the centre and run it under cold water to rid it of any hidden grit. Then slice the leek in half lengthways and finely chop that too, followed by the celery sticks.

Next, heat 1 tablespoon of the olive oil in the casserole and when the oil is hot, brown the chicken breasts on both sides until golden brown. Then transfer the chicken to a plate and now add the rest of the oil to the casserole. Stir in the onions, carrots, leek and celery and cook everything over a low heat, covered with the lid, to allow the vegetables to sweat in their own juices for 10-15 minutes or until they are beginning to soften.

While that is happening, you can prepare the chorizo sausage. Peel the skin off the chorizo and then cut into small dice before stirring it into the vegetables with the pimentón. Turn the heat up to medium and cook everything together for 2-3 minutes to start to draw the fat from the chorizo – you will need to stir constantly to keep everything on the move, to prevent the chorizo from sticking to the bottom of the casserole. Now add the cooked, drained beans (you can throw away the thyme and the bay leaf), garlic, tomatoes, the other bay leaf and the saffron, followed by the hot stock. Season with salt and freshly milled black pepper and give everything a good stir. Place the chicken breasts on top, bring the whole lot to simmering point, then reduce the heat to low and leave to simmer, covered, for 20-25 minutes.

Finally, lift the chicken breasts out on to warmed plates, and stir the parsley into the sauce before spooning it over the chicken. Serve it with a chicory and rocket salad.

Thai Red Curry Chicken
Serves 8

8 part-boned chicken breasts

1 tablespoon groundnut or other flavourless oil

salt

For the curry paste

4 medium, red chillies, deseeded

juice and zest of a lime

1 tablespoon finely chopped lemon grass,

1 inch (2.5 cm) cube of fresh root ginger

4 garlic cloves, peeled

4 Thai shallots, peeled (or normal shallots, if not available)

1 teaspoon shrimp paste

2 tablespoons Thai fish sauce

To garnish

a few sprigs of fresh coriander

2 limes, cut into quarters

This pungent curry paste is speedy to make and freezes well. So, you can make it in bulk, freeze and use it as and when you need it. This means you don't have to shop for small amounts of the ingredients. If you're really short of time, you can use ready-made bought Thai red curry paste.

To make the curry paste, all you do is put everything into a food processor or blender, then switch on to a high speed and blend until you have a rather coarse, rough-looking paste. Remove the paste and keep it covered in the fridge until you need it. About one or two hours before you need to cook the chicken, lay the breasts in a medium, heatproof dish, then take a sharp knife and make four diagonal cuts across each breast. Sprinkle first with a little salt and then with the oil, rubbing the oil well into the chicken. Next, spread the curry paste over the surface of each portion and rub that in well too. Cover with clingfilm and leave on one side in a cool place for the chicken to soak up all the flavours.

To cook the chicken, pre-heat the oven to gas mark 4, 350°F (180°C). Remove the clingfilm, then place the dish on a high shelf and cook for 35-40 minutes, basting with the juices from time to time. Serve the chicken with rice, garnishing with sprigs of coriander and some lime quarters to squeeze over.

Spiced Chicken
Serves 2

2 part-boned chicken breasts, skin on

½ teaspoon sea salt

1 small clove garlic

1 heaped teaspoon ground ginger

1 heaped teaspoon ground turmeric

1 dessertspoon groundnut or other flavourless oil

1 small onion, chopped

7 fl oz (200 ml) half-fat or full-fat crème fraîche

1 heaped tablespoon medium curry powder

a few fresh coriander sprigs, to garnish

Pre-heat the oven to gas mark 4, 350°F (180°C).

This is one of the first recipes I did for London's *Evening Standard*, approximately 30 years ago – it has stood the test of time wonderfully and has even improved with the addition of the crème fraîche.

Begin by placing the salt in a mortar and crush it quite coarsely, then add the garlic and, as you begin to crush it and it comes into contact with the salt, it will break down into a purée. Next, add the ground ginger, turmeric and the oil, and using circular movements, really work all the ingredients together until you have a thick brown paste.

Next, scatter the chopped onion in the middle of a small roasting tin and then, holding one of the chicken breasts in your hand and using a spatula, smear half of the paste over both sides of the chicken breast and then place it on top of the onion before doing exactly the same with the other. Now transfer the tin to the oven and cook the chicken on the middle shelf for 30 minutes.

Meanwhile, in a jug, whisk together the crème fraîche and the curry powder. Then, when the chicken has had its cooking time, spoon the crème fraîche over the chicken breasts and cover the tin with foil before returning it to the oven for a further 30 minutes. I like to serve this with spiced basmati rice and add a few coriander sprigs for a garnish.

Summer

Chicken Salad
with Tarragon and Grapes
Serves 4-6

a 3 lb (1.35 kg) cooked chicken

1 heaped teaspoon chopped
fresh tarragon

4 oz (110 g) seedless green
grapes, halved

5 fl oz (150 ml) mayonnaise

3 fl oz (75 ml) double cream

3 spring onions, finely chopped

1 small crisp lettuce, washed
and patted dry

a few sprigs of watercress,
to garnish

salt and freshly milled
black pepper

Again, this one goes back a long way but stands the test of time perfectly. One of the very nicest salads for a summer day.

First of all, remove the skin from the chicken and slice the flesh into longish pieces, where possible. Then, remove all the chicken from the bones and place the meat in a large bowl, seasoning with salt and pepper.

Next, in a separate bowl, mix the mayonnaise thoroughly with the cream, adding the chopped tarragon and finely chopped spring onions. Now pour the sauce over the chicken, mix it well so that all the chicken pieces get a good coating, then arrange it on a plate of crisp lettuce leaves, scatter over the green grapes and garnish with a few sprigs of watercress.

Chicken and Herb Picnic Pies
Makes 6

For the pastry

1 fl oz (25 ml) milk

3 oz (75 g) pure vegetable fat

8 oz (225 g) strong plain white flour, plus a little extra for dusting

½ teaspoon each dry English mustard, mixed spice and sea salt

a good grating of nutmeg

3 large egg yolks (2 yolks to be used for glazing the pies)

For the filling

1-2 skinless chicken breasts (7 oz/200 g)

¼ teaspoon powdered mace

5 oz (150 g) good-quality pork sausagemeat (I often use skinned sausages)

2 spring onions (including the green parts), finely chopped

½ teaspoon chopped fresh thyme, plus six small sprigs

1 teaspoon chopped fresh sage

1 tablespoon chopped fresh parsley

1 teaspoon lemon juice and ½ teaspoon finely grated zest

1 tablespoon double cream

salt and freshly milled black pepper

You will also need a muffin tin with six cups, each one 3 inches (7.5 cm) across the top and about 1¼ inches (3 cm) deep, lightly greased, a plain 3¼ inch (8 cm) pastry cutter and a small baking sheet.

This one is perfect for food on the move. Take along some radishes and crisp spring onions for an accompaniment and, of course, pickles and chutney.

You need to start by making the filling. So, first of all, cut the chicken into ½ inch (1 cm) pieces, then place them in a bowl, add the mace and season with salt and pepper. Now, in a separate bowl, combine the sausagemeat with the spring onions, the chopped thyme, sage, parsley, lemon juice and zest. Add the cream and mix everything together well.

Pre-heat the oven to gas mark 4, 350°F (180°). Now for the pastry, put the milk and 2 fl oz (55 ml) water into a small saucepan and add the vegetable fat, cut up into small pieces. Place the pan over a gentle heat and simmer until the fat has dissolved. Sift the flour, mustard, mixed spice, sea salt and nutmeg into a large mixing bowl, and mix in 1 of the egg yolks so that it is evenly distributed.

When the fat has completely melted in the liquid, turn up the heat to bring it just up to the boil, and pour it on to the dry ingredients and, using a wooden spoon, mix everything together. Then turn the dough out on to a lightly floured work surface and bring it together with your hands to make a ball. You have to work quickly now, as it's important that the pies go into the tin whilst this dough is still warm. Take two-thirds of the dough and cut this up into 6 equal parts. Roll each of these into a ball and put 1 into each of the holes in the tin. Using your thumb, quickly press each ball flat on to the base and then up to the top edge. Press the pastry over the rim of the top edge; it should overlap by at least ¼ inch (5 mm).

Using a teaspoon, divide half of the sausagemeat among the 6 pies. Then follow this with the chicken and then the rest of the sausagemeat, pressing the filling in firmly as you go. Then roll out the remaining pastry and cut out six 3¼ inch (8 cm) rounds; the pastry will be quite thin, so you may need to sprinkle the work surface with a little extra flour. Next, using a fork, lightly beat the remaining 2 egg yolks together in a small bowl. Then, using a pastry brush, paint some of the egg yolk round the upper edge of the pies and gently press on the lids. Using a small fork, press the rim of each lid against the top of the pie case, make a hole in the top of each pie and glaze with the rest of the yolk. Finally, push a small sprig of thyme into the top of each pie.

Now place the muffin tin on the baking sheet and bake the pies for 30 minutes on the middle shelf. After this time, using oven gloves or a thick cloth, carefully remove the hot pies from the tin and place them directly on to the hot baking sheet, a small round-ended knife is useful for getting the pies out of the tin. Glaze the sides of the pies with the remaining egg yolk and return them to the oven for a further 20 minutes or until the sides and base of the pies are crispy, then leave them to cool on a wire rack. When cold, store in an airtight container in the fridge; they'll keep like this for a couple of days, but bring them to room temperature before eating.

Chicken Basque
Serves 4

a 3 lb 8 oz (1.6 kg) chicken, jointed into 8 pieces

2 large red peppers

1 very large or 2 medium onions

2 oz (50 g) sun-dried tomatoes in oil

2-3 tablespoons extra virgin olive oil

2 large cloves garlic, chopped

5 oz (150 g) chorizo sausage, skinned and cut into ½ inch (1 cm) slices

brown basmati rice measured to the 8 fl oz (225 ml) level in a glass measuring jug

10 fl oz (275 ml) chicken stock

6 fl oz (175 ml) dry white wine

1 tablespoon tomato purée

½ teaspoon hot paprika

1 teaspoon chopped fresh herbs

2 oz (50 g) pitted black olives, halved

½ large orange, peeled and cut into wedges

salt and freshly milled black pepper

You will also need a wide, shallow, flameproof casserole with a domed lid, measuring about 9½ inches (24 cm) at the base; or, failing that, any wide (8 pint/4.5 litre), flameproof casserole.

The delicious combination of chicken and rice, olives and peppers is typical of all the regions around the western Mediterranean but, to my mind, this Spanish version, with the addition of spicy chorizo sausage and a hint of paprika, beats the lot. My interpretation of it also uses dried tomatoes preserved in oil to give it even more character. This recipe will provide a complete supper for four from the same pot – it needs nothing to accompany it!

Start by seasoning the chicken joints well with salt and pepper. Next, slice the red peppers in half and remove the seeds and pith, then slice each half into 6 strips. Likewise, peel the onion and slice into strips of approximately the same size. The sun-dried tomatoes should be drained, wiped dry with kitchen paper and then cut into ½ inch (1 cm) pieces.

Now heat 2 tablespoons of olive oil in the casserole and, when it is fairly hot, add the chicken pieces – 2 or 3 at a time – and brown them to a nutty golden colour on both sides. As they brown, remove them to a plate lined with kitchen paper, using a draining spoon. Next, add a little more oil to the casserole, with the heat slightly higher than medium. As soon as the oil is hot, add the onion and peppers and allow them to brown a little at the edges, moving them around from time to time, for about 5 minutes. After that, add the garlic, chorizo and sun-dried tomatoes and toss these around for a minute or two until the garlic is pale golden and the chorizo has taken on some colour. Next, stir in the rice and, when the grains have a good coating of oil, add the stock, wine, tomato purée and paprika. As soon as everything has reached simmering point, turn the heat down to a gentle simmer. Add a little more seasoning, then place the chicken gently on top of everything (it's important to keep the rice down in the liquid). Finally, sprinkle the herbs over the chicken pieces and scatter the olives and wedges of orange in among them.

Cover with a tight-fitting lid and cook over the gentlest possible heat for about 50 minutes-1 hour or until the rice is cooked but still retains a little bite. Alternatively, cook in a pre-heated oven at gas mark 4, 350°F (180°C) for 1 hour.

Barbecued Chicken with an Apricot Glaze
Serves 6

18 small-to-medium chicken drumsticks

a glass of white wine

For the apricot barbecue glaze

2 large fresh apricots

2 rounded tablespoons dark soft brown sugar

2 fl oz (55 ml) Worcestershire sauce

2 fl oz (55 ml) light soy sauce

1 tablespoon grated fresh ginger

1 rounded teaspoon ground ginger

a few drops of Tabasco sauce

2 tablespoons tomato purée

1 clove garlic

freshly milled black pepper

This is a sauce that's suitable for all meats but particularly chicken drumsticks. One important point is that drumsticks need pre-baking in a pre-heated oven for 15 minutes just before glazing and barbecuing.

Begin by placing the apricots in a small saucepan with enough water to cover them, then bring them up to simmering point and simmer for 2 minutes. Now drain off the water and, as soon as they are cool enough to handle, slip off the skins (protect your hands with a cloth if they're too hot). Then halve and stone them and place the flesh in a blender or food processor, together with all the other glaze ingredients. Whiz everything to a purée and the sauce is ready. All you do now is arrange the drumsticks in a shallow dish, pour the glaze over them – turning the pieces of chicken so that each one gets a good coating – then cover and leave in a cool place until you're ready to cook.

Pre-heat the oven to gas mark 4, 350°F (180°C). When you light the charcoal, pre-cook the chicken drumsticks for 15 minutes, then, when your charcoal is at the right heat, brush the drumsticks with the glaze and cook for about 5 minutes on each side about 3 inches (7.5 cm) from the coals. What we like to do sometimes is scrape any sauce that's left in the dish into a small saucepan, add a glass of white wine to it, and bring it all up to simmering point to give some extra sauce. Serve the barbecued chicken with a crisp salad and some very robust red wine!

Grilled Lemon Chicken Kebabs with Gremolata
Serves 2

2 boneless chicken breasts, skin on

juice of 1 lemon, plus 1 teaspoon grated lemon zest

3 thick slices of lemon, cut into quarters

2 fl oz (55 ml) olive oil

1 clove garlic, crushed

1 dessertspoon chopped fresh oregano

1 teaspoon white wine vinegar

2 bay leaves, torn in half

salt and freshly milled black pepper

For the gremolata

1 clove garlic, finely chopped

1 heaped teaspoon grated lemon zest

1 tablespoon chopped fresh parsley

You will also need two wooden skewers, about 10 inches (25.5 cm) long. Alternatively, use metal skewers.

This is what we all need – something easy to prepare, really fast to cook that also tastes exceptionally good. Serve with rice or salad or both, or, instead of the rice, warm crusty bread to dip into the juices.

Begin by chopping each chicken breast into 5 chunky pieces, leaving the skin on, and place them in a bowl, along with the lemon juice and zest, oil, garlic, oregano, white wine vinegar and plenty of seasoning. Cover and leave to marinate overnight in the fridge or for a few hours – or for as much time as you have.

When you are ready to cook the chicken, if using wooden skewers, soak them in hot water for 30 minutes to prevent them from burning. Then pre-heat the grill to its highest setting at least 10 minutes ahead, and first thread half a bay leaf on to the first skewer, followed by a quarter-slice of lemon, then a piece of chicken. Carry on alternating the lemon and chicken until you have used 5 pieces of chicken, finishing off with a lemon quarter and another half of a bay leaf at the end and making sure you pack everything together as tightly as possible. Repeat with the second skewer, then place them both on a grill rack, and underneath the rack place a heatproof dish to catch the juices. The kebabs should be 4 inches (10 cm) from the grill, and as they cook you need to baste them with the marinade juices. They will need 10 minutes on each side to cook through and become nice and dark and toasted at the edges.

While they're under the grill, mix the gremolata ingredients together and have it ready. When the chicken is done, transfer it to a serving plate and keep warm. Now put the rest of the marinade, plus the basting juices, in a saucepan and boil to reduce to a syrupy consistency, which will take about 2 minutes. Pour this over the chicken and sprinkle the gremolata all over as it goes to the table.

6 whole cloves

15 black peppercorns

1½ oz (40 g) unsalted cashew nuts, halved

2 medium onions, finely sliced

4 oz (110 g) fresh shelled peas, or frozen and defrosted

1½ teaspoons salt, or to taste

2 tablespoons lime juice

You will also need two large frying pans, one with a close-fitting lid.

cook for another 2-3 minutes. After that, add the coconut mixture, give everything a stir, and cook for a further 2-3 minutes. Now add the peas, salt and 15 fl oz (425 ml) hot water, bring it all up to a gentle simmer, then cover with the lid. Turn the heat to low and let everything cook very gently for 8 minutes; use a timer here, and don't lift the lid.

Now add the chicken to the thickened coconut sauce and simmer gently for 10 minutes or so to heat it through completely. When the rice is ready, remove the pan from the heat, take the lid off and cover the pan with a cloth for 10 minutes before serving. Finally, remove the pieces of cinnamon from the rice, sprinkle in the lime juice and the finely chopped coriander leaves, then fork the rice gently to separate the grains. Serve the chicken on a bed of rice, garnished with the reserved whole coriander leaves.

Curried Chicken Salad
Serves 6

a medium cooked chicken,
or 1 lb (450 g) leftover
cooked chicken

½ tablespoon Madras curry paste

1½ oz (40 g) whole blanched
almonds

2½ fl oz (65 ml) mayonnaise

1½ fl oz (40 ml) natural yoghurt

1 tablespoon mango chutney with
any bits of mango finely chopped

1½ oz (40 g) raisins

1½ oz (40 g) dried, ready-to-eat
apricots, quartered

3 spring onions, sliced thinly
(including the green parts)

3 oz (75 g) baby leaf salad

1 dessertspoon fresh coriander
leaves, to garnish

salt and freshly milled
black pepper

Pre-heat the oven to gas mark 4,
350°F (180°C).

This is unbelievably easy if you buy ready-cooked chicken. It's also a great way of using up leftover chicken and is perfect for serving as part of a buffet.

Spread the almonds out on a baking sheet and toast in the pre-heated oven for 8 minutes, using a timer. Let them cool for a couple of minutes, then roughly chop them.

Now, if using a whole chicken, strip all the meat from it, discarding the skin and bones. Cut the chicken into bite-sized pieces and place them in a mixing bowl. Then, in a small bowl, mix the mayonnaise and yoghurt with the curry paste and mango chutney, then pour this sauce over the chicken. Next, add the raisins, apricots, about two-thirds of the almonds and about three-quarters of the spring onions. Mix everything together thoroughly, taste and season with salt and freshly milled black pepper, then cover and chill till needed.

When you are ready to serve, place the salad leaves in the base of a serving dish and spoon the chicken over the top, heaping it up to give it some height. Then scatter the reserved almonds and spring onions and the coriander leaves over the top.

Roast Chicken
with Grape and Herb Stuffing
Serves 4

a 4 lb (1.8 kg) chicken

2 oz (50 g) butter,
at room temperature

salt and freshly milled
black pepper

For the stuffing

6 oz (175 g) seedless grapes,
or ordinary grapes, halved and
deseeded

1 tablespoon chopped fresh
parsley

2 teaspoons chopped fresh
tarragon

3½ oz (95 g) butter

1 medium onion, finely chopped

4 oz (110 g) fresh breadcrumbs

4 cloves garlic, crushed

salt and freshly milled
black pepper

For the gravy

1 rounded tablespoon plain flour

10 fl oz (275 ml) dry white wine

10 fl oz (275 ml) good chicken
stock

salt and freshly milled
black pepper

Pre-heat the oven to gas mark 5,
375°F (190°C).

This is good for a family Sunday lunch in summer with fresh shelled broad beans and buttered new potatoes.

First, make the stuffing. Melt ½ oz (10 g) of the butter in a small saucepan and cook the finely chopped onion for about 5 minutes or until softened, then add the remaining butter and allow it to melt. Now transfer the onion and the buttery juices to a bowl, add the breadcrumbs, then stir in the crushed garlic, chopped parsley, tarragon and grapes. Taste and season with salt and pepper.

Next, loosen the breast skin of the chicken a little to make a pocket for the stuffing. Place the stuffing in the pocket but don't overfill – if you do, the skin will burst when cooking. Secure the skin flap underneath with a small skewer. Season the chicken all over with lots of salt and pepper, then rub it all over with the 2 oz (50 g) butter, and cover the breast with buttered foil.

Place the chicken in a roasting tin and cook for approximately 1 hour, 20 minutes, basting the meat with the buttery juices every 20 minutes or so. Remove the foil half an hour before the end of the cooking time to brown the breast. To test if the chicken is cooked, pierce the thickest part of the thigh with a thin skewer: if cooked, the juices will run golden and clear. Drain the chicken thoroughly and keep warm while you make the gravy.

Carefully tilt the roasting tin and pour off some of the excess fat – you need to leave about 1-1½ tablespoons of fat behind. Then put the tin over direct low heat turned fairly low when the juices begin to sizzle, and blend in the flour. Keep stirring and allow the flour to brown before gradually adding the wine and the stock to make a thin gravy. Taste and season with salt and pepper. Carve the chicken and serve, passing the gravy round separately.

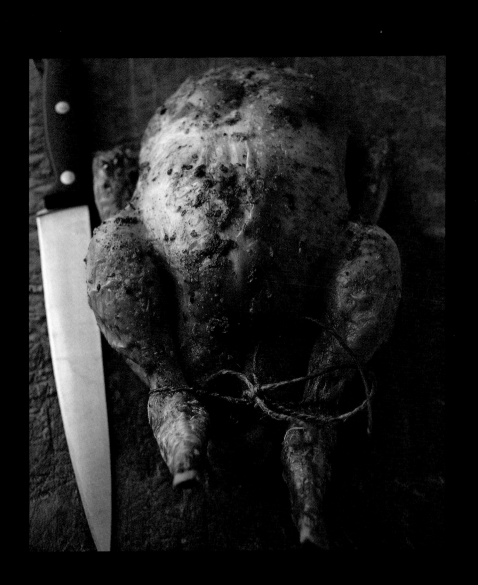

Oven-baked Chicken with Garlic and Parmesan
Serves 4

a 3 lb 8 oz (1.6 kg) chicken, jointed into 8 pieces or a mixture of 8 thigh and leg portions

4 large cloves garlic

1½ oz (40 g) Parmesan, grated

2 large eggs

2 oz (50 g) butter

4 tablespoons olive oil

2 oz (50 g) fresh breadcrumbs

2 heaped tablespoons finely chopped fresh parsley

sea salt and freshly milled black pepper

You will also need a roasting tin large enough to hold the chicken in one layer.

This is excellent picnic food. Small chicken joints are so easy to transport and have the advantage of being easy to eat without knives and forks when you get there.

First of all, arrange the chicken joints in a shallow dish in a single layer to marinate. Then place the garlic cloves in a mortar with 1 heaped teaspoon sea salt and crush the garlic to a purée. Now add this to the eggs in a bowl, season with some pepper and whisk well with a fork before pouring the whole lot over the chicken joints. Cover the dish with clingfilm and leave in a cool place or the fridge for a minimum of four hours, turning the chicken over halfway through.

Pre-heat the oven to gas mark 4, 350°F (180°C), and pop the shallow roasting tin containing the butter and oil into the oven to pre-heat as well. Meanwhile, combine the breadcrumbs with the Parmesan, parsley and a little seasoning together on a plate, and spread out some absorbent kitchen paper. Remove the chicken from the fridge, take one piece at a time and carefully sit it in the crumb mixture, patting and coating it all over with crumbs (trying not to disturb the egg and garlic already clinging to it).

Next, remove the tin with the hot fat in it from the oven and add the chicken pieces, baste well and bake on a high shelf for 20 minutes. Then turn the chicken pieces over and give them another 20 minutes, before finally pouring off the excess fat from the tin and giving them another 5 minutes. Drain them on more kitchen paper, leave to cool and when cold wrap the pieces individually in foil for transportation.

Chicken Kebabs Marinated with Whole Spices and Yoghurt, and Fresh Coriander Chutney
Serves 4

4 boneless, chicken breasts
(about 6 oz/175 g each), skin on

½ large red onion, halved
and separated

8 fresh green chillies, halved and
deseeded

4 bay leaves, cut in half

olive oil, to sprinkle

lime quarters, to serve

salt and freshly milled
black pepper

For the marinade

1 teaspoon cumin seeds

1½ teaspoons coriander seeds

12 cardamom pods

1 rounded tablespoon each
turmeric and grated root ginger

3 cloves garlic, crushed

½ teaspoon sea salt

1 tablespoon groundnut or other
flavourless oil

10 fl oz (275 ml) thick
natural yoghurt

For the fresh coriander chutney

¾ oz (20 g) fresh coriander leaves

2 tablespoons lime juice

1 fresh green chilli, halved
and deseeded

1 clove garlic

½ teaspoon sugar

You will also need four wooden
skewers, 10 inches (25.5 cm) long.
Alternatively, use metal skewers.

Yoghurt as a marinade does wonders for chicken, making it deliciously tender. This is great barbecue food – the charcoal really does add an extra dimension – but these kebabs can also be grilled very successfully. Serve with raw red onion and tomato salad.

Begin by dry-roasting the cumin and coriander seeds and the cardamom pods in a small pan over a medium heat for about 1 minute, or until the seeds begin to jump. When they have cooled, remove the seeds from the cardamom pods and, using a pestle and mortar, crush them with the cumin and coriander seeds. Next, add the turmeric, ginger, garlic and salt and mix everything well.

Now cut each chicken breast into five pieces, place them in a bowl and toss first in groundnut oil, then in the spice mixture, mixing everything around so it gets an even coating. Next, add all but 1 tablespoon of the yoghurt (reserve this for the chutney). Give everything a good stir and press the chicken pieces down into the marinade. Cover with clingfilm pressed on to the surface, and refrigerate for a few hours or, even better, overnight.

To make the chutney, simply whiz everything, including the reserved 1 tablespoon yoghurt, together in a blender, then pour into a bowl and leave aside for 2-3 hours to allow the flavours to develop.

When you are almost ready to cook the kebabs, if you're using wooden skewers, soak them in hot water for 30 minutes (to prevent them burning). Now light the barbecue or pre-heat the grill to its highest setting for 10 minutes. Next, thread half a bay leaf on to a skewer, then a piece of chicken, a piece of onion and half a chilli. Carry on alternating the chicken, onion and chilli until you have used up five pieces of chicken per kebab, and finish with half a bay leaf. Make sure you pack everything as tightly as possible, then season, lay the kebabs on a grill rack and sprinkle with a little olive oil. Put a heatproof dish lined with foil under the rack and grill the kebabs for 10 minutes on each side, about 4 inches (10 cm) away from the source of the heat, or simply grill over a barbecue. To serve, slip the chicken off the skewers, using a fork to ease the pieces off (and a cloth to protect your hand), and serve, garnished with lime quarters, and the chutney handed round separately.

Chicken with Sherry Vinegar and Tarragon Sauce
Serves 4

a 3 lb 8 oz (1.6 kg) chicken, jointed into 8 pieces, or you could use 4 part-boned chicken breasts

5 fl oz (150 ml) good-quality sherry vinegar

2 tablespoons fresh tarragon leaves, plus 8 small sprigs of fresh tarragon, to garnish

2 tablespoons olive oil

12 shallots

4 cloves garlic

15 fl oz (425 ml) medium-dry Amontillado sherry

1 heaped tablespoon crème fraîche

salt and freshly milled black pepper

You will also need a large, roomy frying pan, 9 inches (23 cm) in diameter.

This is my adaptation of a classic French dish called *poulet au vinaigre*. It's very simple to make: the chicken is flavoured with tarragon leaves and simmered in a mixture of sherry vinegar and medium sherry, without a lid, so that the liquid cooks down to a glossy, concentrated sauce. Serve with some well chilled fino sherry as an apéritif.

First of all, heat the oil in the frying pan and season the chicken joints with salt and pepper. Then, when the oil begins to shimmer, fry the chicken in two batches to brown well: remove the first batch to a plate while you tackle the second. Each joint needs to be a lovely golden brown colour. When the second batch is ready, remove it to the plate to join the rest. Then add the shallots to the pan, brown these a little, and finally, add the garlic cloves to colour slightly.

Now turn the heat down, return the chicken pieces to the pan, scatter the tarragon leaves all over, then pour in the vinegar and sherry. Let it all simmer for a bit, then turn the heat to a very low setting, so that the whole thing barely bubbles, for 45 minutes. Halfway through, turn the chicken pieces over to allow the other sides to sit in the sauce. When they're ready, remove them to a warm serving dish, right side up, along with the shallots and garlic.

The sauce will by now have reduced and concentrated, so all you do is whisk the crème fraîche into it, taste it and season as required, then pour the sauce all over the chicken and scatter with the sprigs of tarragon. This is lovely served with tiny new potatoes tossed in herbs and some fresh shelled peas.

Chicken with Lemon Sauce
Serves 4

a 4 lb (1.8 kg) chicken

3 oz (75 g) softened butter

1 lemon, plus 1 dessertspoon lemon juice

1 teaspoon chopped fresh tarragon

salt and freshly milled black pepper

For the sauce

about 10 fl oz (275 ml) chicken stock, preferably home-made

1 tablespoon plain flour

grated zest of ½ lemon

1 tablespoon lemon juice

5 fl oz (150 ml) half-fat or full-fat crème fraîche

You will also need a solid-based, flameproof roasting tin, 9 x 11 inches (23 x 28 cm), and 2 inches (5 cm) deep.

Pre-heat the oven to gas mark 6, 400°F (200°C).

Chicken and lemon sauce was in every recipe book in the Seventies but then seemed to lose its popularity. But we have re-visited my old recipe and I have to say it still tastes extremely good.

First of all, reduce the stock down to 5 fl oz (150 ml) to give a concentrated flavour. This should be done in a wide saucepan, without a lid, boiling vigorously.

Next, prepare the chicken for roasting by mixing the butter with ¼ teaspoon of salt, some freshly milled pepper and the lemon juice. Add the tarragon, then spread this mixture evenly all over the chicken. Now cut the lemon into quarters and place these inside the chicken. Next, place the chicken in a roasting tin and cover the breast with buttered foil. Roast for 1¼-1½ hours, basting the chicken quite often with the buttery juices. Remove the foil from the breast during the last half hour.

When the chicken is ready, remove it to a warm plate and cover with foil. While the chicken is 'relaxing' you can make the sauce. Tilt the roasting tin and remove most of the fat, which you will see separates quite clearly from the juices – you need to leave behind about 2 tablespoons.

Now place the roasting tin over direct heat turned to fairly low, and when the juices begin to sizzle, blend in the flour and stir vigorously until you have a smooth paste and then gradually add the stock, lemon zest and juice. Bring to the boil, stirring all the time, simmer for 2-3 minutes, then add the crème fraîche and season to taste with salt and pepper. Carve the chicken and serve with the sauce poured over.

Autumn

Oven-baked Chicken in Maple Barbecue Sauce
Serves 4

4 chicken thighs and 4 drumsticks, or a medium chicken, jointed into 8 pieces

1 tablespoon olive oil

1 dessertspoon lemon juice

1 medium onion, finely chopped

salt and freshly milled black pepper

For the sauce

2 tablespoons pure maple syrup

3 fl oz (75 ml) red wine

4 tablespoons Japanese soy sauce

2 tablespoons red wine vinegar

1 heaped tablespoon tomato purée

1 heaped teaspoon ground ginger

1 heaped teaspoon mustard powder

2 cloves garlic, crushed

1½ teaspoons Tabasco sauce

To finish

2 fl oz (55 ml) red wine

a few sprigs of watercress

You will also need a shallow roasting tin, 8 x 12 x 2 inches (20 x 30 x 5 cm).

Although the chicken does take about 50 minutes to cook, there is actually very little work involved here. You can, if you like, brush the chicken pieces with the oil and lemon juice well in advance; just cover it with clingfilm and leave in the fridge.

First, mix the olive oil with the lemon juice, place the chicken pieces in the roasting tin with the chopped onion tucked among them. Season with a little salt and freshly milled black pepper and brush the chicken pieces with the oil and lemon juice. When you're ready to cook the chicken, pre-heat the oven to gas mark 6, 400°F (200°C), then pop the chicken in on a high shelf of the oven and let it cook for 25 minutes exactly.

Meanwhile, combine all the sauce ingredients in a jug and, using a small whisk, blend everything thoroughly. Then, when the 25 minutes are up, remove the chicken from the oven, pour off any surplus fat from the corner of the tin and pour the sauce all over, giving everything a good coating.

Now back it goes into the oven for about another 25 minutes (you will need to baste it twice during this time). After that, remove the roasting tin from the oven and place it over direct heat turned to medium.

Then pour in the extra 2 fl oz (55 ml) of red wine, stir it into the sauce, let it just bubble for about 1 minute, then serve the chicken with the sauce spooned over. Garnish with a few sprigs of watercress.

Chicken Feuilletés
Serves 4

For the filling

1 lb (450 g) boneless, skinless chicken thighs

1 oz (25 g) butter

1 small onion, finely chopped

6 rashers dry-cure streaky bacon, rind removed, cut into ¼ inch (5 mm) strips

1 oz (25 g) flour

10 fl oz (275 ml) chicken stock

2 oz (50 g) chestnut mushrooms, finely sliced

2 fl oz (55 ml) crème fraîche or double cream

1½ tablespoons finely chopped fresh parsley

salt and freshly milled black pepper

For the pastry

9 oz (250 g) block of fresh or frozen and defrosted puff pastry

2 large egg yolks, beaten

You will also need a lightly greased baking sheet, 10 x 14 inches (25.5 x 35cm), and a tape measure.

This is good, homely, comfort food but, served in individual portions, it's elegant enough to serve at a supper party. It's also incredibly easy to make, especially if you use fresh or frozen bought puff pastry.

First of all, you need to trim the chicken into even-sized pieces – roughly ½ inch (1 cm) cubes. Then melt the butter in a medium, deep-sided frying pan and fry the chopped onion over a medium heat until it has turned pale gold – about 4 minutes. Then, using a draining spoon, remove it to a plate. Now turn the heat up to high and add the strips of bacon and fry these, tossing them around a few times, for about 4 minutes, until they are really crisp. After that, transfer the bacon to join the onion on a plate and start to fry the chicken in the bacon fat. You'll need to do this in three batches, and each batch should take about 3-4 minutes to turn golden on all sides. Now return the onion and bacon and all the chicken to the frying pan. Then, using a wooden spoon, and keeping the heat at medium, sprinkle in the flour and stir it in to soak up all the juices.

After that, add the chicken stock a little at a time, stirring as you add until all the stock has been incorporated. Then, as it comes to simmer, it will have thickened to a creamy sauce. At this stage, add the mushrooms, season well and then let it simmer at the lowest possible heat, uncovered, for 30 minutes, giving it a stir from time to time. Then, finally, stir in the crème fraîche or cream and the parsley, taste to check the seasoning and then leave it aside until it is completely cooled. Chill in the fridge.

All this can be done well ahead of time, but when you want to make the feuilletés, pre-heat the oven to gas mark 6, 400°F (200°C). Allow the pastry to come to room temperature – this will take about 10 minutes, then roll it out until it measures 16 x 16 inches (40 x 40cm) and then trim it to give four 7 x 7 inch (18 x 18 cm) squares. Gather up the trimmings and reserve these until later. Now divide the cold filling among the four pieces of pastry, placing it in the centre.

Next, brush the edges with the beaten egg yolk, pull up the opposite corners to meet in the centre so that what you have is in fact an envelope. Then pinch the seams together carefully, as you don't want them to burst open. Now make a small hole in the centre of each one to allow the steam to escape, then re-roll the pastry trimmings quite thinly and cut them into leaf shapes, making veins in the leaves with the back of a knife.

Then arrange the leaves to decorate the parcels. You can make the feuilletés up to this stage well in advance and chill them. Either way, they will need to go on a greased baking sheet, then brush the whole lot thickly with beaten egg yolk and bake on a high shelf in the oven for 20-25 minutes or until they are a rich golden brown. All this needs is a lightly cooked green vegetable or a salad.

Chicken with Roasted Lemons, Red Onion, Thyme and Garlic
Serves 4

a 3 lb (1.35 kg) chicken

1 large, red onion, peeled and cut into 6 wedges through the root

1 tablespoon fresh thyme leaves and a few small sprigs

6 cloves garlic
(no need to peel them)

2 tablespoons olive oil

1 large lemon, quartered, plus a squeeze of lemon juice for the sauce

10 fl oz (275 ml) dry white wine

2 tablespoons crème fraîche

salt and freshly milled black pepper

You will also need a solid-based, flameproof roasting tin,
9 x 11 inches (23 x 28 cm), and 2 inches (5 cm) deep.

Pre-heat the oven to gas mark 6, 400°F (200°C).

Something lovely happens to lemons when they're roasted – they lose some of their sharp edge and taste more mellow.

Begin by taking the chicken from the fridge about an hour before you intend to cook it (if it's a hot day, give it about 30 minutes only), and remove the string that holds the legs of the bird together so that the joints are loose – this will take the chill off the bird and help it to cook in the shorter time.

Now put 1 tablespoon of the olive oil in the roasting tin and toss the onion, lemon and garlic in it. Then push everything to the sides of the tin and place the chicken in the middle. Rub the rest of the olive oil all over the skin. Then arrange the onion wedges, lemon and garlic cloves around the chicken.

Season well with salt and black pepper and then scatter the thyme leaves and the small sprigs of thyme over everything in the tin. Now roast the chicken for an hour, basting it once or twice, and then transfer it to a carving board, along with the red onions, lemon and garlic. Cover it with foil and let it rest for 20 minutes.

Meanwhile, using a tablespoon, skim off the excess fat from the juices in the roasting tin, then place the tin over direct heat, add the wine and let the whole lot bubble and reduce to about half its original volume. Stir the crème fraîche in next, adding a small squeeze of lemon juice, bring it back to simmering point and taste and check the seasoning. Then carve the chicken and place on to warm plates, making sure everyone has a piece of onion and lemon and some garlic. Add any juices to the sauce and finally, spoon some sauce over the chicken and serve the leftover sauce in a jug. You can squeeze the garlic pulp out of the cloves as you eat it, and scrape off the lemony flesh from the skins.

Chicken Puttanesca
Serves 4

4 part-boned chicken breasts
(about 8 oz/225 g each), skin on

2 tablespoons extra virgin olive oil

2 cloves garlic, crushed

1 fresh red chilli, deseeded and
finely chopped

14 oz (400 g) tinned Italian
chopped tomatoes

1 rounded tablespoon
tomato purée

6 oz (175 g) pitted black olives,
roughly chopped

1 heaped tablespoon capers,
rinsed and drained

1 tablespoon chopped fresh basil,
plus a few extra sprigs, to garnish

12 oz (350 g) dried spinach
tagliatelle, to serve

salt and freshly milled
black pepper

You will also need a 10 inch
(25.5 cm), solid frying pan that's
not too shallow.

I have long been a fan of the Italian puttanesca sauce for serving with various kinds of pasta. What I've discovered, though, is this variation. This lovely, gutsy sauce is also supremely good with chicken that's been sautéed first, then gently simmered in the sauce to absorb all the flavours. No need to miss out on the pasta either, as green tagliatelle is the perfect accompaniment.

Begin by heating the oil in the frying pan until it's very hot. Wipe the chicken breasts with kitchen paper, season them with salt and pepper, then add them to the hot oil and fry them over a medium heat until they are a rich golden colour on both sides. This will take about 5 or 6 minutes. Then transfer the chicken to a plate and add the garlic and chilli to the pan and fry these briefly for about 30 seconds.

After that, add the tomatoes, tomato purée, olives, capers, chopped basil and some seasoning. Stir everything well, bringing it up to a gentle simmer, then return the chicken breasts to the pan, skin side up, pushing them well down into the sauce and basting a little over the top. Now simmer for 40-45 minutes, uncovered, until the chicken has cooked and the sauce has reduced and thickened.

About 15 minutes before the end of the cooking time, put a large pan of salted water on to heat and bring it up to the boil – this will take about 10 minutes. Then boil the tagliatelle – put a timer on it and give it 5 minutes. After that, quickly drain and serve the chicken with the sauce spooned over, the tagliatelle on the side, and garnish with the fresh sprigs of basil.

Chicken Cacciatora
Serves 4

a 3 lb (1.35 kg) chicken, jointed into 8 pieces

1 tablespoon olive oil

2 largish onions, thickly sliced

1 lb 8 oz (700 g) ripe red tomatoes

2 large cloves garlic, crushed

1 tablespoon tomato purée

1 tablespoon fresh rosemary leaves, bruised and finely chopped, plus a few small sprigs

1 bay leaf

10 fl oz (275 ml) dry white wine

1 tablespoon white wine vinegar

salt and freshly milled black pepper

You will also need a 6 pint (3.5 litre), lidded, flameproof casserole.

This is my version of the famous Italian classic — best made in the autumn when there's a glut of red, ripe, full-flavoured tomatoes, but it's still good in winter, as there are now some well-flavoured varieties available. Either way, the tomatoes need to be very red and ripe. This is good served with noodles, rice, tagliatelle or a simple vegetable.

First of all, heat the oil in the casserole over a high heat and season the chicken joints with salt and pepper. Then, when the oil gets really hot and begins to shimmer, fry the chicken – in two batches – to brown it well on all sides: remove the first batch to a plate while you tackle the second; each joint needs to be a lovely golden brown colour all over. When the second batch is ready, remove it to join the rest. Now add the onions to the casserole, turn the heat down to medium and cook for 8-10 minutes, or until they are softened and nicely browned at the edges.

Meanwhile, skin the tomatoes. To do this, pour boiling water over them and leave them for exactly 1 minute before draining and slipping off their skins (protect your hands with a cloth if they are too hot), then chop them quite small.

When the onions are browned, add the garlic to the casserole, let this cook for about 1 minute, then add the tomatoes, tomato purée, rosemary, bay leaf, white wine and white wine vinegar. Now add some seasoning and bring it up to the boil, then let it bubble and reduce (without covering) to about half its original volume, which will take about 20 minutes. Now add the chicken pieces, stir them around a bit, then put the lid on and allow to simmer gently for 40 minutes, until the chicken joints are cooked through.

Chicken Breasts with Wild Mushroom and Bacon Stuffing and Marsala Sauce
Serves 4

4 boneless, skinless chicken breasts (each about 5 oz/150 g)

½ oz (10 g) dried porcini mushrooms

6 oz (175 g) open-cap mushrooms, finely chopped

3 oz (75 g) streaky bacon or sliced pancetta

1 oz (25 g) butter, plus extra for greasing

1 medium onion, finely chopped

1 fat garlic clove, crushed

1 heaped teaspoon chopped fresh sage leaves

a grating of nutmeg

salt and freshly milled black pepper

For the sauce

5 fl oz (150 ml) dry Marsala, plus about a spoonful more if it's too thick

1 teaspoon groundnut or other flavourless oil

reserved bacon or pancetta

1 shallot, chopped

3 small mushrooms, finely sliced

1 teaspoon chopped fresh sage leaves

¾ dessertspoon plain flour

soaking liquid from porcini

salt and freshly milled black pepper

You will also need four 10 inch (25.5 cm) squares of foil.

This is a very simple way to deal with four boneless chicken breasts. The use of wild porcini mushrooms combined with the beautifully rich flavour of Marsala wine in the sauce turns them into something quite unusual and special.

First, you need to soak the porcini mushrooms, so pop them into a jug, pour 5 fl oz (150 ml) of boiling water over them and leave them to soak for 20 minutes. After that, strain them in a sieve placed over a bowl and squeeze every last bit of liquid out of them because you are going to need it for the sauce. Now melt the butter in a good solid frying pan, finely chop the bacon or pancetta and cook half of it in the hot butter until golden and crisp, and remove it to a plate. Then add the chopped onion to the pan and fry that gently for about 5 minutes to soften.

While that is happening, chop the strained porcini finely and then add these to the pan, along with the garlic, sage and finely chopped open-cap mushrooms, a little nutmeg and the cooked bacon or pancetta. Stir well to get everything coated with the butter, then, as soon as the juices start to run out of the mushrooms, reduce the heat to very low and let the whole lot cook gently, without covering, until all the juices have evaporated and all you have left is a thick mushroom paste. This will take about 30 minutes in all. After that, remove it from the heat, taste, and season well with salt and freshly milled black pepper, then allow it to get completely cold.

Now take each of the chicken breasts and remove the silvery sinew from the back. Fold back the fillet, making a deeper cut if necessary, so it opens out almost like a book, then season the chicken. Next, spread a quarter of the mushroom mixture over one of the breasts, fold back the flap and then roll it up lengthways like a Swiss roll. When they are all filled, lay each chicken breast on a lightly buttered piece of foil. Wrap each in its foil, folding over the ends to seal. At this stage the parcels should be chilled for at least an hour to firm up. When you're ready to cook them, pre-heat the oven to gas mark 8, 450°F (230°C). Place the chicken parcels on a baking sheet and cook for 20 minutes. Then remove them from the oven and allow them to rest in the foil for 10 minutes before serving.

While the chicken is cooking, you can make the sauce. First add the oil to the pan in which you cooked the mushroom filling, then gently fry the remaining bacon or pancetta and the shallot for about 5 minutes, then add the sliced mushrooms and chopped sage, stir and continue to cook for about 1 minute, by which time the juices of the mushrooms will begin to run.

Next, stir in the flour to soak up the juices, then gradually add the porcini soaking liquid, followed by 5 fl oz (150 ml) Marsala and give a good seasoning of salt and freshly milled black pepper. Keep stirring until it bubbles and thickens, then turn the heat down and add a spoonful more of Marsala, if you think it's too thick. Now let the sauce cook very gently for about 20 minutes. To serve, unwrap each parcel on to a plate and cut each into 4 pieces – at an angle to show the stuffing. Then pour the sauce over or around each one and serve straightaway.

Chicken in Cider
Serves 4

a 3 lb (1.35 kg) chicken, jointed into 8 pieces

1 pint (570 ml) dry cider

2 tablespoons groundnut or other flavourless oil

2 medium onions, chopped

1 clove garlic, chopped

6 rashers unsmoked streaky bacon

1 sprig of fresh thyme

1 bay leaf

8 oz (225 g) dark-gilled mushrooms, sliced

1 oz (25 g) plain flour
and 1 oz (25 g) softened butter combined to make a paste

salt and freshly milled black pepper

You will also need a 6 pint (3.5 litre), lidded, flameproof casserole.

Pre-heat the oven to gas mark 4, 350°F (180°C).

This is a lovely recipe for autumn and is great served with crisp, buttered jacket potatoes and spiced red cabbage.

First of all, heat the oil in the casserole over a high heat and season the chicken joints with salt and freshly milled black pepper. Then, when the oil gets really hot and begins to shimmer, fry the chicken, in two batches to brown it well on all sides: remove the first batch to a plate while you tackle the second; each joint needs to be a lovely golden-brown colour all over. When the second batch is ready, remove it to join the rest.

Now fry the onions and garlic for 5 minutes or so. Next, the bacon, which should be fried to melt the fat a little, then return everything to the casserole. Throw in the thyme and bay leaf, and now pour in the cider.

Bring it all to simmering point, then cover with the lid and let it simmer gently for 1 hour. At the end of that time add the mushrooms and simmer for a further 5-7 minutes or until the mushrooms are cooked.

Have ready the plain flour mixed to a smooth paste with the butter, and when the chicken is cooked, using a draining spoon, transfer the chicken to a warm serving dish. Next, add the butter and flour paste to the liquid and bring back to simmering point, stirring all the time. Pour the thickened sauce over the chicken and serve immediately.

Thai Green Curry with Chicken
Serves 4-6

a 1 lb (450 g) cooked chicken, sliced into shreds

2 x 400 ml tins coconut milk (you will only need 1½ tins for the recipe; you can freeze the leftover amount for use later on)

For the green curry paste

6-8 whole green bird's-eye chillies

1 lemon grass stalk, sliced thinly and soaked for 30 minutes in 2 tablespoons lime juice

1 rounded teaspoon thinly shredded kaffir or normal lime peel

1 inch (2.5 cm) piece peeled fresh galangal or ginger

1 heaped teaspoon chopped fresh coriander stalks

½ teaspoon each roasted ground cumin and coriander seeds

3 garlic cloves

5 Thai or normal shallots, peeled

1 teaspoon shrimp paste

For the finished sauce

3-4 dessertspoons Thai fish sauce

1 teaspoon palm or soft brown sugar

3 dessertspoons fresh green peppercorns or green peppercorns in brine, drained

7 kaffir lime leaves, if you can find them

½ mild red chilli, deseeded and cut into hair-like shreds

1 oz (25 g) fresh basil leaves, preferably Thai, torn

This recipe was inspired by The Oriental's Cookery School in Bangkok. The unique flavours of Thai cooking are so simple - and because you can use a good-quality cooked chicken from the supermarket - this recipe is actually easy.

The curry paste can be made well ahead of time and there's absolutely no work involved if you have a food processor or a blender because all you do is simply pop all the curry paste ingredients in and whiz it to a paste (stopping once or twice to push the mixture back down from the sides on to the blades). In Thailand, of course, all these would be pounded by hand with a pestle and mortar, but food processors do cut out all the hard work. What you need to end up with is a coarse paste, but don't worry if it doesn't look very green – that's because I have cut the chilli content; in Thailand they use about 35! If you want yours to be green, then this is the answer! Your next task is to prepare all the rest of the ingredients.

To make the curry, first place the tins of coconut milk on a work surface, upside down. Then open them and inside you will see the whole thing has separated into thick cream and thin watery milk. Divide these by pouring the milk into one bowl and the cream into another. Next, place a large flameproof casserole or a wok, without any oil in it, over a very high heat and then as soon as it becomes really hot, add three-quarters of the coconut cream. What you do now is literally fry it, stirring all the time so it doesn't catch. What will happen is it will start to separate, the oil will begin to seep out and it will reduce. Ignore the curdled look – this is normal. You may also like to note that when the cream begins to separate you can actually hear it give off a crackling noise.

Next, add the curry paste and three-quarters of the coconut milk, which should be added a little at a time, keeping the heat high and letting it reduce down slightly. Stay with it and keep stirring to prevent it sticking. Then add the Thai fish sauce and sugar, stir these in and then add the shredded chicken and the peppercorns. Stir again and simmer everything for about 4-5 minutes until the chicken is heated through. Then just before serving, place the lime leaves one on top of the other, roll them up tightly and slice them into very fine shreds, then add them, along with the red chilli and torn basil leaves.

Crunchy Pistachio-coated Drumsticks
Serves 4

8 chicken drumsticks,
skin removed

4 oz (110 g) shelled pistachio nuts

3 tablespoons groundnut or other
flavourless oil

1½ tablespoons lemon juice

3 oz (75 g) plain flour

1½ tablespoons medium
curry powder

¼ teaspoon salt

2 heaped teaspoons fresh
coriander leaves

pinch of cayenne pepper

1 large egg, beaten

3 tablespoons milk

freshly milled black pepper

You will also need a very shallow
baking tin, approximately 10 x 14
inches (25.5 x 35.5 cm).

This recipe also works very well using salted peanuts instead of the pistachios. The chicken has a crunchy coating with a slightly oriental flavour and is popular with both children and adults. This recipe is best started the day before you want to eat the chicken, so it has time to marinate.

First of all, lay the drumsticks in a dish, mix 1½ tablespoons of the oil and the lemon juice together and pour this over the chicken. Then leave the drumsticks to marinate overnight, or for at least 8 hours, turning them over once or twice during this period.

To make the coating, mix the flour, curry powder, the salt and some pepper together in a shallow dish. When you are ready to cook, toss the drumsticks in the flour mixture – a few at a time – until well coated on all sides. Tap off the surplus flour, then lay them on a plate, reserving the unused flour for later.

Now pre-heat the oven to gas mark 7, 425°F (220°C). Place the nuts, coriander leaves, 1½ tablespoons of the reserved flour and the cayenne in a food processor and blend until you have a mixture chopped minutely small, then transfer this to a plate.

After that, beat the egg and milk together in a bowl. Then take each drumstick and dip it once more in the remaining seasoned flour, then into the egg mixture, and finally, into the pistachio mixture. Return the coated drumsticks to their plate and keep cool until needed. To cook, place the baking tin containing the remaining 1½ tablespoons of oil in the oven to pre-heat, then add the drumsticks to the hot oil (making sure they don't touch each other), baste well and bake on a high shelf for 15 minutes. Then pour off the oil and give them 5 more minutes to get really crisp. Drain on kitchen paper and serve.

Chicken Saltimbocca
Serves 2

2 chicken breasts
(about 6 oz/175 g each)

6 slices Parma ham
(about 3 oz/75 g in total)

8 large fresh sage leaves

8 fl oz (225 ml) dry Marsala

1 teaspoon olive oil

salt and freshly milled
black pepper

You will also need eight
cocktail sticks.

Saltimbocca is a classic Italian dish, which is usually made with thin veal but it also works beautifully with chicken. The chicken is quickly sautéed and then the whole thing is finished with a rich, dark Marsala wine sauce.

First of all, prepare the chicken breasts, which need to be flattened out. So, place one of them between 2 large pieces of clingfilm and gently pound it, using a rolling pin, being careful not to break the meat. It needs to be flattened out to a shape measuring about 6 x 7 inches (15 x 18 cm), $\frac{1}{8}$-$\frac{1}{4}$ inch (3-5 mm) thick. Repeat this with the second chicken breast, between 2 fresh pieces of clingfilm. Then cut each flattened chicken breast into 4 pieces measuring about 3 x 3$\frac{1}{2}$ inches (7.5 x 9 cm) each.

Next, you need to separate the slices of Parma ham and cut a 1$\frac{1}{2}$ inch (4 cm) strip off the end of each slice. (You'll need these smaller pieces of ham to finish off 2 of the chicken pieces.) Now place a piece of ham on each slice of chicken, folding and creasing it up to fit, if necessary, then divide the 6 smaller pieces of ham between the last 2 chicken pieces. Finally, top each one with a sage leaf and secure the whole thing together with a cocktail stick. Then season each piece on both sides with salt and freshly milled black pepper.

Next, measure the Marsala into a small saucepan and heat it gently until it begins to bubble. While that's happening, cook the chicken: heat the oil in a medium frying pan over a fairly high heat and when it's really hot, put in half the pieces of chicken, sage side down, reduce the heat to medium and fry for 2-3 minutes, until crisp and golden. Then turn them over and give the other side about a minute before removing them to a warm serving dish. Do the same with the remaining pieces and when they're done, keep them warm with the others.

Now pour the warmed Marsala into the frying pan, turn the heat right up again and let it bubble and reduce to a syrupy sauce, which should take 4-5 minutes. Return the chicken pieces to the pan and turn in the sauce. Serve on warmed plates (not forgetting to remove the cocktail sticks!) with the syrupy sauce poured over.

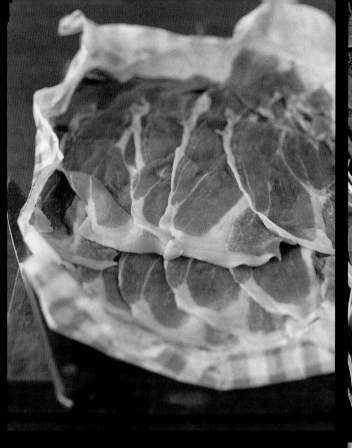

Chicken Waldorf Salad
Serves 4

a 2 lb 4 oz (1 kg) cooked chicken

4 sticks of celery (4 oz/110 g), chopped

8 spring onions, chopped (including the green parts)

2 oz (50 g) walnut halves, roughly chopped

6 oz (175 g) seedless black grapes, halved

a few lettuce leaves

sprigs of watercress, to garnish

For the dressing

1 teaspoon sea salt

2 cloves garlic

2 teaspoons chopped fresh tarragon

2 rounded tablespoons mayonnaise

2 heaped dessertspoons natural yoghurt

freshly milled black pepper

This would make a lovely main course salad, served on a bed of crisp lettuce. The new season's 'wet' walnuts are perfect for this recipe if you can get hold of them.

Begin by stripping the skin from the chicken and discarding it. Then remove the flesh from the bones and slice it into longish, 1 inch (2.5 cm) thick pieces, and place these in a large bowl. Next, add the chopped celery to the bowl, together with the spring onions and chopped walnuts.

Now for the dressing: place the salt in a mortar and crush it quite coarsely, then add the garlic and, as you begin to crush it and it comes into contact with the salt, it will quickly break down to a purée. Next add the tarragon, mayonnaise and yoghurt with a few twists of freshly milled pepper and blend everything together thoroughly. Pour the dressing over the salad and toss everything together well to get a good coating of the dressing. Arrange some lettuce leaves in a large, shallow serving dish, pile the chicken salad on top, sprinkle the grapes all over, and, if you like, garnish with sprigs of watercress.

Chicken Breasts
with Stem Ginger Sauce
Serves 4

4 chicken breasts

4 pieces of preserved stem ginger, finely chopped

4 dessertspoons preserved stem ginger syrup (from the jar)

2 teaspoons grated fresh root ginger

2 tablespoons groundnut or other flavourless oil

1 large onion, chopped small

2 cloves garlic, crushed

a knob of butter

4 fl oz (120 ml) dry white wine or dry cider

2 tablespoons natural yoghurt

4 spring onions, finely sliced on the diagonal

salt and freshly milled black pepper

Pre-heat the oven to gas mark 5, 375°F (190°C).

Preserved stem ginger is a wonderful storecupboard standby and I always have a jar of it handy. It keeps indefinitely so it doesn't matter if you don't use it often and there's never any waste. This is good served with a mixed salad of watercress, rocket and baby spinach.

Start off by heating the oil in a medium saucepan and soften the onion and garlic in it for about 5 minutes. Meanwhile, place the chicken breasts in a medium roasting tin. Then pierce the chicken with a skewer or small sharp knife in several places, this is to allow the ginger to seep down inside.

Now spoon the ginger syrup over the chicken, rubbing it in with your hands. Next, sprinkle the grated root ginger over and rub that in as well. Season the chicken with salt and pepper, then pour the onion, garlic and oil from the saucepan over it, and place a small knob of butter on top of each one.

Bake the chicken in the oven for about 25 minutes, basting it with the juices about halfway through. When it's cooked, remove it to a warmed serving plate, then place the tin over direct medium heat. Add the wine (or cider) and chopped stem ginger, stir and let it bubble down to a syrupy sauce. Then, off the heat, stir in the yoghurt. Pour the sauce over the chicken and sprinkle with the spring onions.

Winter

Chicken Baked with 30 Cloves of Garlic
Serves 4

a 4 lb (1.8 kg) chicken

30 cloves garlic, unpeeled
(3-4 heads)

½ oz (10 g) butter

1 dessertspoon olive oil

6 small sprigs fresh rosemary,
plus 1 heaped tablespoon
rosemary leaves, bruised
and chopped

10 fl oz (275 ml) white wine

salt and freshly milled
black pepper

For the huff paste

8 oz (225 g) plain flour, plus a little
extra for dusting

You will also need a lidded,
flameproof casserole large enough
to hold the chicken comfortably –
about 8 pints (4.5 litres).

Pre-heat the oven to gas mark 6,
400°F (200°C).

Before you cry off this one, remember that garlic, simmered gently for 1¼ hours, mellows deliciously, losing much of its pungency. I have to admit it's probably not the thing to eat before a first date, but otherwise it's utterly sublime. In this recipe, a huff paste (you don't eat this) is used to make a perfect seal for the lid of the casserole, ensuring that all the juices and fragrances remain intact. It's made in moments, but if you want to you could use foil instead.

First of all, dry the chicken as much as possible with kitchen paper and season it well. Next, melt the butter and oil in the casserole, then, keeping the heat fairly high, brown the chicken carefully on all sides. This will seem a bit awkward, but all you do is protect your hands with a cloth and hold the chicken by its legs, turning it into different positions until it is a good golden colour all over; this will take 10-15 minutes in all. After that, remove the chicken from the casserole, add the cloves of garlic and rosemary sprigs, toss these around, then replace the chicken and sprinkle the chopped rosemary all over. Next, pour the wine all around it and let it gently come up to simmering point.

Meanwhile, place the flour in a bowl and add 5 fl oz (150 ml) cold water – it should be enough to make a soft but not sticky dough – then divide the dough into 4 and roll each piece into a cylinder about 9 inches (23 cm) long on a lightly floured surface. Now position these all around the rim of the casserole – it doesn't matter what they look like. Place the casserole lid carefully on top, pressing down gently and making sure there are no gaps. Alternatively, simply place a double sheet of foil over the casserole before putting the lid on.

Now place the casserole in the oven and cook for 1¼ hours, then remove the lid and let the chicken continue to cook for another 10 minutes, to re-crisp the skin. Next, remove the chicken from the casserole and allow it to rest for 10 minutes before carving. Serve the carved chicken with the garlic cloves alongside and the cooking juices poured around it. The idea is to squash the garlic cloves with a knife to release all the creamy pulp and, as you eat, dip the pieces of chicken into it.

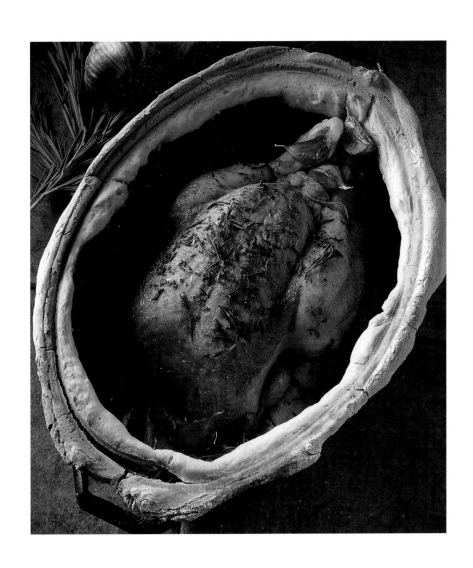

Marinated Chicken with Honey and Ginger, served with Mango and Sultana Salsa
Serves 4

4 chicken breasts (6 oz/175 g each), skin on

salt and freshly milled black pepper

For the marinade

2 tablespoons runny honey

1 inch (2.5 cm) piece of fresh root ginger, peeled and finely grated

1 teaspoon ground ginger

2 cloves garlic, crushed

zest and juice of ½ lime

salt and freshly milled black pepper

For the salsa

1 medium or ½ large mango

2 oz (50 g) sultanas

zest and juice of 1 lime

½ red pepper, deseeded and chopped

½ medium red onion, finely chopped

1 medium green chilli, deseeded and finely chopped

To garnish

½ oz (10 g) fresh coriander leaves

You will also need an ovenproof dish, 6 x 8 inches (15 x 20 cm), and 2 inches (5 cm) deep.

This is a quick and easy recipe that's helpful for busy people because it needs to be prepared ahead, preferably the day before. I like to serve it with potatoes that have been brushed with saffron oil after par-boiling, before being roasted at the same temperature as the chicken for 40-50 minutes or until really crunchy. For the saffron oil, mix a generous pinch of saffron stamens with a tablespoon of olive oil.

Begin this by making two cuts in each chicken breast, about ¼ inch (5 mm) deep, then place the chicken breasts neatly in the ovenproof dish. Now combine all the marinade ingredients in a bowl, whisking them together, then pour this over the chicken breasts, turning them around in the marinade to get them well coated. You now need to cover the dish with clingfilm and leave it in the fridge overnight.

Next, place the sultanas for the salsa with the lime zest and juice in a small bowl so they can plump up overnight. Cover them with clingfilm and store in the fridge.

When you are ready to cook the chicken, pre-heat the oven to gas mark 7, 425°F (220°C). Then remove the clingfilm from the chicken and baste each breast with the marinade. Bake on a high shelf of the oven (or the next one down if you are roasting potatoes at the same time) for 20-30 minutes.

While the chicken is cooking, remove the skin from the mango, using a potato peeler or sharp knife. Then slice all the flesh away from the stone and chop it into small pieces – about ¼ inch (5 mm) dice. Then add it to the sultanas, along with the remaining salsa ingredients, and garnish, just before serving, with the coriander leaves. Serve the cooked chicken with some of the salsa spooned over and the rest served separately, along with a bowl of roasted potatoes, which have been sprinkled with a little salt.

Oriental Chicken Stir-fry with Broccoli and Cashew Nuts
Serves 2-3

3 skinless chicken breasts
(1 lb/450 g)

1 heaped tablespoon cornflour

½ teaspoon five-spice powder

2 dessertspoons Japanese
soy sauce

4 oz (110 g) shiitake mushrooms

4 oz (110 g) broccoli florets

4 spring onions

3 tablespoons groundnut
or other flavourless oil

4 oz (110 g) cashew nuts

1 small onion, finely chopped

2 cloves garlic, crushed

2 teaspoons fresh ginger, peeled
and grated

1 teaspoon salt

4 tablespoons rice wine or dry
sherry, mixed with 2 tablespoons
Japanese soy sauce

You will also need a wok or a very
large frying pan with a lid.

The great thing about stir-fries is speed and you could ring the changes by replacing broccoli with sliced sugar snaps, and shiitake mushrooms with any other mushroom. It's also quite a good idea to have a kitchen timer handy to time all the bits and pieces.

First, you need to cut the chicken into strips, which should be about ¼ inch x 2 inches (5 mm x 5 cm). Then place them in a large bowl and toss with the cornflour and five-spice powder so that all the strips get an even coating. Next, sprinkle in the soy sauce and give the whole thing a really good toss. Then cover the bowl and leave it aside for 30 minutes while you prepare all the other ingredients.

The shiitake mushrooms should be cut into thin slices and the broccoli needs to have the heads cut – also in thin slices, and the stalks cut into very thin diagonal slices. What you do with the spring onions is chop the white part quite small and the green part into very thin shreds.

When you are ready to cook the stir-fry, first heat 1 tablespoon of the oil in the wok or frying pan and, when it's very hot, fry the cashew nuts for 45-60 seconds until they are a lovely golden brown colour. Keep them on the move all the time, then remove them to a plate, using a draining spoon. Now add another tablespoon of oil and, again, when it becomes really hot, keep the heat high and stir-fry the chicken in two batches, giving each batch 2-3 minutes, until it turns crisp and golden and becomes cooked through. As the chicken cooks, remove it to a plate and keep warm.

Now add the last tablespoon of oil, this time keeping the heat at medium. Stir-fry the chopped onion, garlic and ginger for about 2 minutes. Then turn the heat up to high again, add the mushrooms and broccoli and stir-fry these for a further minute, tossing them around all the time so they come in contact with the heat on all sides. Return the chicken and cashew nuts to join the rest, season with the salt, then add the rice wine (or dry sherry and soy mixture). Turn the heat down to medium, then add the chopped spring onions, cover with a lid, and let it all cook for just 1 minute. Serve immediately on a bed of rice noodles or plain steamed rice, with the rest of the finely shredded raw spring onions sprinkled over.

Crisp-fried Chicken Breasts with Melting Cheese and Chives
Serves 4

4 skinless chicken breasts (6 oz/175 g each)

4 oz (110 g) Lancashire, Wensleydale or Cheddar

1 tablespoon finely chopped chives

1 oz (25 g) flour seasoned with salt and pepper

2 large eggs, beaten

3 oz (75 g) fresh white breadcrumbs

2-3 tablespoons groundnut or other flavourless oil

salt and freshly milled black pepper

The cheese you use for this can vary. It is lovely with a mild and crumbly cheese, such as Lancashire or Wensleydale, but if you prefer a highly flavoured cheese, try a mature Cheddar. It is good served with a green salad with lots of watercress in it.

First of all, take each of the chicken breasts and using a small, very sharp knife, make a cut to form a pocket in each one lengthways. Then crumble the cheese and mix it with the chives and fill each of the pockets with a quarter of the cheese mixture.

Next, dust the chicken breasts with seasoned flour, then coat them in beaten egg and then roll each one in breadcrumbs, pressing the breadcrumbs firmly all round to get an even coating.

Now heat 2 tablespoons of the oil in a large frying pan and, keeping the heat at medium, cook the chicken breasts for 10 minutes on each side, by which time they will be golden brown and cooked through, adding a little more oil, if necessary. Drain them briefly on kitchen paper and sprinkle with salt and freshly milled black pepper before serving.

Coq au Vin
Serves 6-8

a 5 lb (2.25 kg) chicken,
jointed into 8 pieces

1¼ pints (725 ml) red wine
or dry cider

1 oz (25 g) butter

1 tablespoon groundnut or other
flavourless oil

8 oz (225 g) unsmoked bacon
lardons or cubed pancetta

16 shallots or button onions

2 cloves garlic, crushed

2 sprigs fresh thyme

2 bay leaves

8 oz (225 g) small, dark-gilled
mushrooms

1 rounded tablespoon softened
butter and 1 tablespoon plain flour,
combined to make a paste

chopped fresh parsley, to garnish

salt and freshly milled
black pepper

You will also need a 6 pint
(3.5 litre), flameproof casserole,
wide and shallow enough to take
the chicken joints in one layer.

A truly authentic *coq au vin* is made, obviously, with a cock bird. In Britain we make a less authentic adaptation, but it makes a splendid dinner party dish. The results are different but every bit as delicious if you use cider instead of wine, but it must be dry cider.

Melt the butter with the oil in a large frying pan, and fry the chicken joints, skin side down, until they are nicely golden, then turn them and colour the other side. You may have to do this in three or four batches – don't overcrowd the pan. As they are ready, remove the joints from the pan with a draining spoon, and place them in the casserole. This should be large enough for the chicken pieces to be arranged in one layer yet deep enough so that they can be completely covered with liquid later.

Now brown the lardons or pancetta also in the frying pan and add them to the chicken, then finally brown the shallots or onions a little and add them too. Next, place the crushed cloves of garlic and the sprigs of thyme among the chicken pieces, season with freshly milled pepper and just a little salt, and pop in a couple of bay leaves. Pour in the wine or dry cider, put a lid on the pot and simmer gently for 45-60 minutes or until the chicken is tender. During the last 15 minutes of the cooking, add the mushrooms and stir them into the liquid.

Remove the chicken, bacon, onions and mushrooms and place them on a warmed serving dish and keep warm. Discard the bay leaves and thyme at this stage.

Now bring the liquid to a fast boil and reduce it by about one-third. Next, add the butter and flour paste to the liquid. Bring it to the boil, whisking all the time, until the sauce has thickened, then serve the chicken with the sauce poured over. If you like, sprinkle some chopped parsley over the chicken and make it look pretty. This is lovely with creamy mashed potatoes.

Chicken with Whole Spices
Serves 4

a 4 lb (1.8 kg) chicken, jointed into 8 pieces

2 cloves garlic, crushed

1 dessertspoon grated fresh root ginger or 1 heaped teaspoon ground ginger

2 teaspoons ground turmeric

1½ tablespoons groundnut or other flavourless oil

salt and freshly milled black pepper

For the spice sauce

¾ teaspoon whole cumin seeds

1 teaspoon whole coriander seeds

8 whole cardamom pods

1 oz (25 g) butter

½ tablespoon groundnut or other flavourless oil

2 onions, very finely chopped

1 medium green pepper, deseeded and finely chopped

2 dried red chillies, deseeded and very finely chopped

1 bay leaf, crumbled

5 oz (150 g) natural yoghurt, mixed with 2 fl oz (55 ml) hot water

salt

You will also need an oblong roasting tin or ovenproof dish large enough to take the chicken pieces in a single layer.

This is another perennial favourite that has stood the test of time. Serve it with spiced pilau rice with mango chutney.

Prepare the chicken a few hours before cooking. Arrange the pieces in the roasting tin or dish. In a small bowl, mix together the crushed garlic, ginger and turmeric with the oil. Now, with a sharp knife, make several incisions in the chicken pieces, season with salt and pepper, then coat them as evenly as possible with the oil and spice mixture. Leave in a cool place (but not in the fridge) so that the flavours penetrate.

When you're ready to cook the chicken, pre-heat the oven to gas mark 6, 400°F (200°C). Place the tin or dish on the highest shelf, uncovered, and cook for about 20 minutes or until the chicken pieces are a nice golden colour.

Meanwhile, prepare the whole spices. First of all, place them in a thick-based frying pan over a medium heat for about 1 minute until they turn one shade darker, tossing them to keep them on the move. This warming of the spices helps to draw out all the flavour. Now grind them and crush finely, either with a pestle and mortar. You can discard the cardamom pods but make sure you keep all the seeds from inside.

Next, melt the butter and oil together in a frying pan. Add the onions and green pepper, and cook for 5 minutes. Now add the crushed spices, chillies and crumbled bay leaf, stir and cook for a further 5 minutes. Take the pan off the heat, stir in the yoghurt and water and add a little salt. Now pour this mixture all over the chicken pieces, cover the tin with a double sheet of foil, and bake for 30 minutes with the heat reduced to gas mark 4, 350°F (180°C), then remove the foil and let it cook for a further 10 minutes.

Marinated Chicken Satays
with Peanut Satay Sauce
Serves 6 as a starter or 4 as a main course

4 skinless chicken breasts
(6 oz/175 g each)

For the marinade

1 tablespoon clear honey

1 tablespoon Japanese soy sauce

a few drops of Tabasco

1 clove garlic, crushed

1 teaspoon grated fresh ginger

For the sauce

4 oz (110 g) natural, roasted
peanuts

1½ tablespoons groundnut or other
flavourless oil

3 shallots, finely chopped

1½-2 red chillies, deseeded
and chopped

1 teaspoon grated fresh ginger

2 cloves garlic, crushed

2 tablespoons lime juice

1½ tablespoons Japanese
soy sauce

1 tablespoon light soft brown sugar

1 tablespoon coriander leaves

You will also need about 10-12
bamboo skewers, 8 inches
(20 cm) long. Alternatively, use
metal skewers.

These are no trouble to make with ready-boned and skinned chicken breasts, and the sauce can be whizzed up in seconds. These are excellent served as part of a winter buffet.

First of all, prepare the marinade, which simply means putting all the ingredients in a bowl and whisking them thoroughly together. Then, to prepare the chicken, take each chicken breast and remove the little fillet. Now cut this in half lengthways. Next, slice the main breast horizontally so that you then have 2 thinner, flat slices. Then cut each of these into 3 or 4 strips lengthways: you should get about 8 or 9 strips from each chicken breast. Now gather up all the little strips and put them into the marinade, tossing and stirring them well until they get a good coating. Next, cover the bowl and leave it aside in a cool place for at least 30 minutes – although two or three hours would be better.

To prepare the sauce, first heat the groundnut oil in a frying pan and, over a medium heat, soften the shallots for about 3 minutes. Then add the chillies, ginger and garlic and fry these for a further 1½ minutes. Next, add the peanuts and toss them around for about 1½ minutes. After that, remove the pan from the heat and allow everything to cool. As soon as it's cool, tip everything into a food processor with the rest of the sauce ingredients and 3 tablespoons of water and whiz until roughly chopped, but do be careful not to overprocess, as the sauce needs to have some texture. After that, transfer it to a serving bowl.

All the above can be done well in advance, but before you cook the satays, if you are using the bamboo skewers, don't forget to soak them in hot water for about 30 minutes to prevent them from burning. Then, when you're ready to cook the chicken, pre-heat the grill to its highest setting for 10 minutes.

Meanwhile, thread the strips of chicken – about 3 or 4 pieces – on to each skewer, threading them in a loose S shape (see left). Then pop them under the grill about 3 inches (7.5 cm) from the heat source, giving them about 3-4 minutes on each side. Serve on warm plates with the peanut sauce handed round separately.

Chicken in the Pot
Serves 4

a 3 lb (1.35 kg) chicken

3 tablespoons olive oil

8 oz (225 g) unsmoked lardons
or chopped pancetta

12 shallots or button onions

4 medium carrots, peeled
and cut into 1 inch (2.5 cm) chunks
or 6 whole baby carrots

4 small turnips, peeled and
quartered

1 clove garlic, crushed

10 fl oz (275 ml) dry white wine

15 fl oz (425 ml) chicken stock

1 small bunch of parsley stalks

a few celery leaves (if you happen
to have them)

2 sprigs of fresh thyme

1 bay leaf

8 oz (225 g) dark-gilled
mushrooms, sliced

a paste made with 1 rounded
tablespoon softened butter
and 1 tablespoon plain flour

salt and freshly milled
black pepper

You will also need a 6 pint
(3.5 litre), flameproof casserole.

Pre-heat the oven to gas mark 6,
400°F (200°C).

This is my version of the famous *poule au pot* associated with Henri IV of France, whose ambition was that every family in his kingdom might be able to afford to eat this dish every Sunday. I'm really pleased to be able to re-introduce a great classic.

First, heat 1 tablespoon of the oil in the casserole, then fry the lardons or pancetta a little with the shallots or button onions. When they have coloured a bit, remove them with a slotted spoon and keep them on one side.

Now, add the rest of the oil and when it is fairly hot, fry the chicken whole. This will seem a bit awkward, but all you do is protect your hands with a cloth and hold the chicken by its legs, turning it into different positions until it is a good golden colour all over; this will take 10-15 minutes in all, then remove it from the casserole. Next, fry the carrots, turnips, and crushed garlic for about 5 minutes, stirring them all around so that they brown slightly. Now put the bacon and onions back in the pan. Push everything to the sides and sit the chicken in the centre. Next, pour in the wine and stock, add the parsley and celery leaves, tied in a bundle (if using celery leaves), plus the thyme, bay leaf and salt and pepper. Bring to simmering point, then transfer the casserole to the oven (the casserole should be without a lid, but place a piece of foil over the chicken breast) and let it cook for 30 minutes, uncovering and basting the chicken breast now and then with the surrounding stock. After 30 minutes, remove the foil, add the sliced mushrooms, then bake for another 30 minutes, again basting fairly often with the juices. When the chicken is cooked, take the casserole from the oven, remove the chicken, drain it well and put it on a warmed serving dish. Surround it with the well-drained vegetables and bacon, and discard the bay leaf and herbs.

Now place the casserole over a direct heat and boil the liquid fiercely to reduce it by about a third. Then whisk in the flour and butter paste, and bring back to the boil, whisking continuously until the sauce thickens. Now taste to check the seasoning, then carve and serve the chicken and vegetables with the sauce poured over them.

Moroccan Baked Chicken with Chickpeas and Rice
Serves 4

a 3 lb 8 oz-4 lb (1.6-1.8 kg) chicken, jointed into 8 pieces, or a mixture of 8 drumsticks and thighs

4 oz (110 g) dried chickpeas

6 fl oz (175 ml) brown basmati rice

1 teaspoon cumin seeds

1 tablespoon coriander seeds

½ teaspoon saffron stamens

2 small, thin-skinned lemons

2 large yellow peppers

2 large onions

2 tablespoons olive oil

1 oz (25 g) fresh coriander

3 cloves garlic, chopped

2 fresh chillies, halved, deseeded and finely chopped

10 fl oz (275 ml) good chicken stock

5 fl oz (150 ml) dry white wine

2 oz (50 g) pitted black olives

2 oz (50 g) pitted green olives

salt and freshly milled black pepper

You will also need a wide, shallow, flameproof casserole, about 9 inches (23 cm) across the base.

Pre-heat the oven to gas mark 4, 350°F (180°C).

Chicken pieces simmered with chickpeas, peppers and olives in a saffron-flavoured rice with coriander and lemons. This is one of my most popular recipes, because, I imagine, everything needed for a meal for four people is cooked in one large cooking pot with no extra vegetables needed. If you can get hold of them, use a tablespoon of chopped preserved lemon instead of the lemon slices.

There are two ways to deal with chickpeas. The easiest is to pop them into a bowl, cover them with cold water and leave them overnight or for a minimum of 8 hours. But, if it slips your mind, what you can do is place them in a saucepan, cover them with cold water and bring them up to the boil for 10 minutes. Then turn off the heat and let them soak for 3 hours. Either way, when you want to start making this recipe, the chickpeas need to be simmered for 20 minutes or until tender.

While they're simmering, place a small frying pan over direct medium heat, add the cumin and coriander seeds and toss them around in a hot pan for about 2-3 minutes or until they start to dance and change colour. Then remove the seeds to a pestle and mortar and crush them coarsely and transfer them to a plate. Next, crush the saffron stamens to a powder with the pestle and mortar, then squeeze out the juice of one of the lemons and add it to the saffron, stirring well.

Now prepare the chicken by seasoning the joints with salt and pepper. Slice the peppers in half, remove the seeds and pith and cut each half into four large pieces. The onions should be sliced roughly the same size as the peppers. Now heat 1 tablespoon of the olive oil in the flameproof casserole and, when it's really hot, brown the chicken pieces on all sides – don't overcrowd the pan; it's best to do it in two batches, four pieces at a time.

After that, remove the chicken pieces to a plate, then add the second table-spoon of oil and turn the heat to its highest setting. When the oil is really hot, add the peppers and onions and cook them in the hot oil, moving them around until their edges are slightly blackened – this should take about 5 minutes – then turn the heat down. Strip the coriander leaves from the stalks, wrap the leaves in a piece of clingfilm and keep them in the fridge. Then chop the coriander stalks finely and add these to the peppers and onions, along with the garlic, chillies, crushed spices, the chickpeas and rice, then give everything a good stir to distribute all the ingredients.

Season well with salt and pepper, then combine the lemon and saffron mixture with the stock and wine, pour it all in to the casserole and stir well. Cut the remaining lemon into thin slices and push these well into the liquid. Now scatter the olives in and, finally, place the pieces of chicken on top of everything. Cover with a tight-fitting lid and place in the pre-heated oven for 1 hour or until the rice and chickpeas are tender. Then, just before serving, scatter the coriander leaves on top and serve straightaway on warmed serving plates.

Chicken Jambalaya
Serves 2-3

2 boneless, skinless chicken thighs (9 oz/250 g in total), cut into bite-sized pieces

4 oz (110 g) chorizo sausage, peeled and cut into ¾ inch (2 cm) pieces

1-2 tablespoons olive oil

1 medium onion, cut into ½ inch (1 cm) slices

2 cloves garlic, crushed

2 sticks celery, trimmed and sliced into ½ inch (1 cm) pieces on the diagonal

1 green chilli, deseeded and finely chopped

1 yellow pepper, deseeded and cut into ½ inch (1 cm) slices

6 fl oz (175 ml) white basmati rice

about 1 pint (570 ml) hot chicken stock

1 teaspoon Tabasco sauce

3 medium tomatoes, dropped into boiling water for 1 minute, then peeled and chopped

1 bay leaf

salt and freshly milled black pepper

For the garnish

1 tablespoon roughly chopped fresh flat-leaf parsley

2 spring onions, trimmed and finely sliced

You will also need a 10 inch (25.5 cm) frying pan with a lid.

Jambalaya is one of the easiest and best rice dishes that owes its origins to the traditional Cajun cooking of America.

First of all, heat the frying pan over a high heat and brown the pieces of chorizo sausage, without adding any fat, then remove them from the pan to a plate and set aside. Then add a tablespoon of the oil and, when it's hot, brown the chicken and transfer that to the plate with the chorizo. Next, fry the onions for 2-3 minutes to brown them a little at the edges, then return the chorizo and chicken to the pan and add the garlic, celery, chilli and sliced pepper. Continue to fry for 4-5 minutes, till the celery and pepper are also softened and lightly tinged brown at the edges, adding a little more oil if you need to.

Now stir in the rice to get a good coating of oil, then add the Tabasco to the pint (570 ml) of hot chicken stock. Next, add the chopped tomatoes and bay leaf to the pan, then pour in the stock. Season with salt and freshly milled black pepper, give it all one stir and push the rice down into the liquid. Now turn the heat to low, put a lid on and let it barely simmer for 20 minutes. Then, check that the rice is cooked and add a little more stock, if necessary. Cover with a lid for 5 more minutes, then serve, garnished with the chopped parsley and spring onions.

Chicken and Leek Pot Pie
Serves 2

2 boneless, chicken breasts, skin on

2 medium leeks

10 fl oz (275 ml) dry cider

2 medium carrots, peeled and cut into ⅛ inch (3 mm) slices

1 bay leaf

1 small sprig of fresh thyme

8 oz (225 g) block of fresh or frozen and defrosted puff pastry

a little flour for dusting

1 small egg, lightly beaten

1 tablespoon finely grated Parmesan, for sprinkling

salt and freshly milled black pepper

For the sauce

10 fl oz (275 ml) milk

¾ oz (20 g) plain flour

¾ oz (20 g) butter

a pinch of cayenne pepper

1 oz (25 g) mature Cheddar, grated

½ oz (10 g) Parmesan, finely grated

a little freshly grated nutmeg

salt and freshly milled black pepper

You will also need a small, round casserole or heatproof dish, 7 x 2½ inches (18 x 6 cm), with a capacity of 1½ pints (850 ml).

This is what I call comfort food – the kind of thing to make on a cold, grey, winter's day. You can vary the vegetables if you like (I quite like it with mushrooms replacing half the leeks).

First, pour the cider into a medium saucepan, along with the carrots, bay leaf, sprig of thyme and some salt and freshly milled black pepper. Bring to simmering point, then cover with a lid, and simmer gently for 5 minutes. Now take the tough green ends off the leeks, then make a vertical split halfway down the centre of each leek and run them under cold water to rid them of any hidden grit. Then slice them in half lengthways and chop into ½ inch (1 cm) slices. Add the chicken and leeks to the pan and simmer covered for a further 10 minutes.

For the sauce, all you do is place the milk, flour, butter and cayenne pepper into a medium saucepan and place it over a gentle heat. Then, using a balloon whisk, begin to whisk while bringing it to a gentle simmer. Whisk continually until you have a smooth, glossy sauce, and simmer very gently for 5 minutes. Then add the cheeses and whisk again, allowing them to melt. Then season with salt, freshly milled black pepper and some freshly grated nutmeg. Next, drain the chicken and vegetables, reserving the liquid, but not the bay leaf and thyme. Now pour the liquid back into the pan, bring it to the boil and reduce to about 2 tablespoons. Meanwhile, skin the chicken and cut it into bite-sized strips.

Pre-heat the oven to gas mark 6, 400°F (200°C). Now stir the cheese sauce into the cider, bring to a simmer, and stir the chicken, carrots and leeks into the sauce, before transferring the whole lot to the dish.

Next, to make a lid, roll the pastry out thinly on a lightly floured surface. Cut out an 9 inch (23 cm) round, then roll out the trimmings and cut a ½ inch (1 cm) strip. Now dampen the edge of the dish with water and press the strip of pastry around the rim. Dampen the strip and carefully lift the pastry lid over the top. Press it firmly over the edge to get a good seal all round, then trim, using a knife. Finally, gather up the trimmings and re-roll them to cut into leaf shapes. Brush the surface of the pie with beaten egg, and arrange the leaves on top. Now, brush the leaves with beaten egg, sprinkle with Parmesan and bake on the baking sheet for 20 minutes.

Traditional Roast Chicken with Apple, Sage and Onion Stuffing
Serves 6-8

For the roast chicken

a 5-6 lb (2.25-2.7 kg) chicken

2 oz (50 g) butter,
at room temperature

8 rashers traditionally cured,
smoked, streaky bacon

salt and freshly
milled black pepper

**For the apple, sage
and onion stuffing**

1 dessert apple, cored
and quartered

1 heaped tablespoon fresh
sage leaves

1 small onion, quartered

4 oz (110 g) fresh white bread,
crusts removed (about 3 slices)

1 tablespoon fresh parsley leaves

reserved chicken livers from the
giblets (use the rest of the giblets
to make the stock for the gravy)

8 oz (225 g) minced pork or
good-quality pork sausagemeat
(I often use skinned sausages)

¼ teaspoon powdered mace

salt and freshly milled
black pepper

You will also need a large,
flameproof roasting tin,
10 x 14 inches (25.5 x 35 cm),
and 2 inches (5 cm) deep.

This is a family roast chicken, moist and succulent for Sunday lunch, with lots of crispy bacon and some very savoury stuffing. Serve with Traditional Chicken Giblet Gravy (you will need to make the stock ahead of time, see page 127), Traditional Bread Sauce and Cranberry, Sage and Balsamic Sauce (see page 128).

If you have a food processor, making stuffing is a doddle: all you do is switch the motor on, add the pieces of bread and process to crumbs, then add the parsley, sage, apple and onion quarters and process till everything is finely chopped. Next, trim any sinewy bits from the chicken livers, rinse under cold water, pat them dry, then add them, together with the pork or sausagemeat, mace and seasoning. Give a few pulses in the processor until it is all thoroughly blended, remove the stuffing from the processor with a spatula, then place in a polythene bag and store in the fridge until it is required. If you're doing this by hand, just finely chop all the ingredients, combine in a bowl and refrigerate as above.

For the chicken, pre-heat the oven to gas mark 5, 375°F (190°C). First of all, the chicken needs to be stuffed, and to do this, you begin at the neck end, where you'll find a flap of loose skin: gently loosen this away from the breast and you'll be able to make a triangular pocket. Pack about two-thirds of the stuffing inside, as far as you can go, making a neat round shape on the outside, then tuck the neck flap under the bird's back and secure it with a small skewer or cocktail stick. Place the remaining stuffing in the body cavity (the fat in the pork will melt and help to keep the bird moist inside). Now place the chicken in the roasting tin and smear the butter over the chicken, using your hands and making sure you don't leave any part of the surface unbuttered.

Season the chicken all over with salt and black pepper, then arrange 7 slices of the bacon, slightly overlapping, in a row along the breast. Cut the last rasher in half and place one piece on each leg. I like to leave the rind on the bacon for extra flavour, but you can remove it if you prefer. Then place the chicken in the oven on the centre shelf and cook for 20 minutes per lb (450 g), plus 10-20 minutes extra – this will be 1 hour 50 minutes to 2 hours for a 5 lb (2.25 kg) bird, or 2 hours 10 minutes to 2 hours 20 minutes for a 6 lb (2.7 kg) bird. The chicken is cooked if the juices run clear when the thickest part of the leg is pierced with a skewer. It is important to baste the chicken at least three times during the cooking – spooning over the juices mingling with the bacon fat and butter helps to keep the flesh succulent.

During the last basting (about half an hour before the chicken is cooked), remove the now crisp bacon slices and keep them warm. If they are not crisp, just leave them around the chicken to finish off. For the final 15 minutes of cooking, hike the heat up to gas mark 7, 425°F (220°C), which will give the skin that final golden crispiness.

When the chicken is cooked it is important to leave it in the warm kitchen (near the oven), covered in foil, for 30 minutes, to allow it to 'relax'. This is because when the chicken is cooking all the juices bubble up to the surface (if you look inside the oven you will actually see this happening just under the skin), and the 'relaxing' allows time for all these precious juices to seep back into the flesh. It also makes it much easier to carve. When you serve the chicken, make sure everyone gets some crispy bacon and stuffing.

Traditional Gravy and Other Sauces

Traditional Chicken Giblet Gravy

Makes about ½ pint (850 ml),
to serve 6-8 people

This is a real chicken-flavoured gravy
to serve with a family roast chicken for
Sunday lunch. Serve with the recipe
for Traditional Roast Chicken with Apple,
Sage and Onion Stuffing on page 124.
You should make the stock ahead of
time to allow it to cool completely
before you need to use it.

For the chicken giblet stock

8 oz (225 g) chicken giblets – fresh or frozen
and thoroughly defrosted

1 medium carrot, roughly chopped

½ onion

a few fresh parsley stalks

a sprig of fresh thyme

1 bay leaf

½ teaspoon black peppercorns

For the gravy

the juices left in the roasting tin
from cooking a roast chicken

2 rounded tablespoons plain flour

about 1½ pints (850 ml) chicken giblet stock,
but the exact amount will depend on how thick
you like your gravy

salt and freshly milled black pepper

Begin by simply placing the giblets,
1½ pints (850 ml) water, carrot, onion,
herbs, peppercorns and a little salt in a
medium saucepan and simmer very
gently with the lid almost on for two
hours. Now strain the stock into a jug, cool
and then chill in the fridge. Any fat on the
surface is easily removed when cold.

To make the gravy, after removing
the chicken from the roasting tin which
it has cooked in, tilt the tin and remove
most of the fat, which you will see
separates quite clearly from the juices –
you need to leave about 2 tablespoons
of fat behind.

Now place the roasting tin over
direct heat turned to fairly low, and
when the juices begin to sizzle, sprinkle
in the plain flour, stirring vigorously till
you get a smooth paste, then add the
giblet stock, little by little, exchanging
the wooden spoon for a whisk.

Whisk the gravy thoroughly until
all the stock is incorporated. Now bring
the whole lot up to simmering point and
season with salt and freshly milled
black pepper. Then pour the piping hot
gravy into a warm serving jug and hand
round separately with the roast chicken.

Traditional Bread Sauce
Serves 8

Traditional bread sauce is one of the great, classic British sauces, but I think it has suffered either from not being made properly or – worst of all – being made from a mix or packet. The real thing is beautifully creamy and the perfect accompaniment to chicken. Leave the milk to infuse for two hours or more before making the sauce.

4 oz (110 g) freshly made white breadcrumbs from a two-day-old white loaf with crusts removed

1 large onion

15-18 whole cloves
or grated nutmeg

1 bay leaf

8 black peppercorns

1 pint (570 ml) creamy milk

2 oz (50 g) butter

2 tablespoons double cream

salt and freshly milled black pepper

Cut the onion in half and stick the cloves in it (how many you use is a personal matter – I happen to like a pronounced flavour of cloves). If you don't like them at all, you can add some freshly grated nutmeg to the milk instead. Place the onion – studded with cloves – plus the bay leaf and the peppercorns, in a saucepan together with the milk. Add some salt, then bring everything up to boiling point. Take off the heat, cover the pan and leave in a warm place for the milk to infuse for two hours or more. When you're ready to make the sauce, remove the onion, bay leaf and peppercorns and keep them on one side. Stir the breadcrumbs into the milk and add 1 oz (25 g) of the butter. Leave the saucepan on a very low heat, stirring now and then, until the crumbs have swollen and thickened the sauce – about 15 minutes.

Now replace the clove-studded onion and again, leave the pan in a warm place until the sauce is needed. Just before serving, remove the onion. Re-heat gently, then beat in the remaining butter and the cream and taste to check the seasoning. Pour into a warm serving jug and stand until needed.

Cranberry, Sage and Balsamic Sauce
Serves 6-8

I love to serve this with traditional roast chicken.

6 tablespoons cranberry jelly

2 dessertspoons chopped fresh sage

3 tablespoons balsamic vinegar

salt and freshly milled black pepper

All you do here is combine everything in a small saucepan and whisk over a gentle heat until the cranberry jelly has melted. Then pour the sauce into a serving jug and leave till needed (it doesn't need re-heating – it's served at room temperature).

How to Carve a Chicken

When a chicken is cooked, the heat in the oven causes all the internal juices to bubble up to the surface just under the skin – sometimes you can see the skin almost flapping with the amount of juice inside it. Because of this you should always allow the bird to rest for at least 15 minutes before carving it, so that all the wonderful juices travel back from whence they came and keep everything lovely and moist. The fibres of the chicken will also relax, and this will make carving easier.

Carving is very easy, provided you have a sharp knife and follow the instructions given below. A lot of people imagine they can't carve very well, but the truth is probably that the knife they are using simply isn't sharp enough. What you really need to do is buy a good-quality carving knife and a sharpening steel and simply practise. I was taught by a butcher, who said knives should be sharpened little and often. I have also found the following advice good for anyone who wants to learn: hold the steel horizontally in front of you and the knife vertically), then slide the blade of the knife down,

allowing the tip to touch the steel, first on one side of the steel and then on the other. If you really can't face it, there are knife sharpeners available.

Insert the knife between the leg and body and remove the thigh and drumstick in one piece (see opposite, top right).

Remove the wing on the same side, then slice the breast (see bottom left).

Repeat this on the other side of the bird. Finally, divide the drumstick and thigh, cutting through the joint so you have two leg portions (see bottom right).

Conversions for Australia and New Zealand

Measurements in this book refer to British standard imperial and metric measurements.

The standard UK teaspoon measure is 5 ml, the dessertspoon is 10 ml and the tablespoon measure is 15 ml. In Australia, the standard tablespoon is 20 ml.

UK large eggs weigh 63-73 g.

Converting standard cups to imperial and metric weights

Ingredients	Imperial/metric
almonds, whole blanched	5 oz/150 g
apricots, dried, ready-to-eat	6 oz/175 g
basil, fresh*	2 oz/50 g
beans, pinto	6 oz/175 g
breadcrumbs, fresh white	3 oz /75 g
broccoli florets	2½ oz/60 g
butter	9 oz/250 g
cashew nuts, whole	5 oz/150 g
Cheddar, grated*	4½ oz/125 g
chicken, cold, cooked, in strips	5 oz/150 g
chickpeas, dried	8 oz/225 g
coconut, creamed	9 oz/250 g
coriander, fresh, leaves	1 oz/25 g
couscous	6½ oz/185 g
flour, plain	4½ oz/125 g
grapes	6 oz/175 g
Gruyère, grated	4½ oz/125 g
lard	9 oz/250 g
lentils, Puy	7 oz/200 g
mozzarella, grated	5 oz/150 g
olives, pitted	4½ oz/125 g
pancetta, chopped/lardons	5 oz /150 g
Parmesan, grated	4 oz/110 g
peanuts	5½ oz/165 g
pistachio nuts	5 oz/150 g
raisins	4½ oz/125 g
peas (shelled), fresh/frozen	5 oz/150 g
rice, basmati, uncooked	7 oz/200 g
rice, short-grain, white, uncooked	8 oz/225 g
rocket leaves*	1½ oz/40 g
sultanas	4½ oz/125 g
tomatoes, fresh, chopped	7 oz/200 g
tomatoes, tinned, chopped	9 oz/250 g
walnuts, halves	4 oz/110 g

* Firmly packed

Liquid cup conversions

Imperial	Metric	Cups
1 fl oz	25 ml	⅛ cup
2 fl oz	55 ml	¼ cup
2¾ fl oz	80 ml	⅓ cup
4 fl oz	125 ml	½ cup
6 fl oz	185 ml	¾ cup
8 fl oz	250 ml	1 cup
10 fl oz	275 ml	1¼ cups
12 fl oz	375 ml	1½ cups
16 fl oz	500 ml	2 cups
1 pint	570 ml	2½ cups
24 fl oz	750 ml	3 cups
32 fl oz	1 litre	4 cups

A few ingredient names

aubergine
eggplant

courgettes
zucchini

Cox's apple
use a small dessert apple

double cream
thick cream

fine green beans
French green beans

pepper, red/yellow/green
capsicum

shallots
eschalots/French shallots

single cream
thin cream

open-cap/dark-gilled mushrooms
flat-cap mushrooms

spring onions
salad onions/shallots

streaky bacon
use sliced pancetta or speck

spinach
English spinach

spring onions
Spanish onions/red onions

tomato purée
tomato paste

Index

Page numbers in italic refer to the photographs.

Apple, sage and onion
stuffing 124, *125*
Apricots
    barbecued chicken with an apricot
    glaze *46*, 47
Avocado
    creamed chicken with
    avocado 25
Bacon
    chicken breasts with wild mushroom
    and bacon stuffing and Marsala
    sauce 82, *83*
Baked chicken
    chicken baked with 30 cloves
    of garlic 98, *99*
    Moroccan baked chicken with
    chickpeas and rice 116, *117*
Balsamic vinegar
    cranberry, sage and balsamic
    sauce, 128, *129*
Barbecued chicken
    with an apricot glaze *46*, 47
Basque 44, *45*
Bread sauce, traditional 128, *129*
Butter beans
    Spanish chicken with
    butter beans, chorizo and
    tomatoes 30, *31*
Cacciatora *78*, 79
Carve a chicken *130*, 131
Cashew nuts
    oriental chicken stir-fry with
    broccoli and cashew nuts 102, *103*
Cheese
    crisp-fried chicken breasts with
    melting cheese and chives 105
    oven-baked chicken with garlic and
    Parmesan 61
Chicken baked with 30 cloves

of garlic 98, *99*
Chicken Basque 44, *45*
Chicken breasts
    chicken breasts with stem ginger
    sauce 94, *95*
    chicken breasts with wild
    mushroom and bacon stuffing and
    Marsala sauce 82, *83*
    crisp-fried chicken breasts
    with melting cheese and
    chives 105
    poached chicken breasts with
    morel mushrooms, cream and
    parsley 20, *21*
    Spanish chicken with
    butter beans, chorizo and
    tomatoes 30, *31*
Chicken cacciatora *78*, 79
Chicken in cider 85
Chicken feuilletés 72, *73*
Chicken and herb picnic
pies 40, *41*
Chicken jambalaya *118*, 119
Chicken kebabs marinated
with whole spices and yoghurt
and fresh coriander
chutney 62, *63*
Chicken and leek pot pie 120, *121*
Chicken with lemon sauce 66
Chicken paprika *28*, 29
Chicken in the pot *114*, 115
Chicken puttanesca 76, *77*
Chicken salad with tarragon and
grapes 38, *39*
Chicken saltimbocca 90, *91*
Chicken with sherry vinegar and
tarragon sauce *64*, 65
Chicken with roasted lemons,
red onion, thyme and
garlic *74*, 75
Chicken Waldorf salad *92*, 93
Chicken with whole spices *108*, 109

Chickpeas
    Moroccan baked chicken with
    chickpeas and rice 116, *117*
Chilli
    Mexican chicken chilli with yellow
    tomato salsa 18, *19*
Chives
    crisp-fried chicken breasts with
    melting cheese and chives 105
Chorizo
    Spanish chicken with
    butter beans, chorizo and
    tomatoes 30, *31*
Chutney
    fresh coriander chutney 62
Cider
    chicken in cider 85
Coconut
    stir-fried chicken with lime and
    coconut *14*, 15
    Thai creamed coconut chicken
    with Thai green rice 52, *53*
Conversion tables 132
Coq au vin 106, *107*
Coriander
    fresh coriander chutney 62
Couscous
    marinated chicken brochettes with
    green couscous 22, *23*
Cranberry, sage and balsamic
sauce 128, *129*
Cream
    poached chicken breasts with
    morel mushrooms, cream and
    parsley, 20, *21*
Creamed chicken with
avocado 25
Crisp-fried chicken breasts with
melting cheese and chives 105
Crunchy pistachio-coated
drumsticks 88, 89
Curried chicken salad *54*, 55

Curries
    curried chicken salad *54*, 55
    Thai green curry with
    chicken 86, *87*
    Thai red curry chicken 33
Drumsticks
    crunchy pistachio-coated
    drumsticks 88, 89
Fast-roast chicken with lemon and
tarragon 8, *9*
Feuilletés 72, *73*
Garlic
    chicken baked with 30 cloves of
    garlic 98, *99*
    chicken with roasted lemons,
    red onion, thyme and garlic *74*, 75
    grilled chicken with lemon, garlic
    and rosemary, served with
    Puy lentils 12, *13*
    oven-baked chicken with garlic and
    Parmesan 61
Ginger
    chicken breasts with stem ginger
    sauce 94, *95*
    marinated chicken with honey
    and ginger, served with mango and
    sultana salsa *100*, 101
Grapes
    chicken salad with tarragon and
    grapes 38, *39*
    roast chicken with grape and herb
    stuffing 58, *59*
Gravy
    traditional chicken giblet
    gravy *126*, 127
Gremolata
    grilled lemon chicken kebabs
    with gremolata 48, *49*
Grilled chicken
    grilled chicken with lemon, garlic
    and rosemary, served with Puy
    lentils 12, *13*

grilled lemon chicken kebabs
with gremolata 48, *49*
Herb-coated chicken with three
mustards 51
Herbs
chicken and herb picnic pies 40, *41*
herb-coated chicken with three
mustards 51
roast chicken with grape and herb
stuffing 58, *59*
Honey
marinated chicken with honey
and ginger, served with mango and
sultana salsa *100*, 101
How to carve a chicken *130*, 131
Huff paste 98, *99*
Jambalaya *118*, 119
Kebabs
chicken kebabs marinated
with whole spices and yoghurt,
and fresh coriander chutney 62, *63*
grilled lemon chicken kebabs
with gremolata 48, *49*
Leeks
chicken and leek pot
pie 120, *121*
Lemon
chicken with lemon sauce 66
fast-roast chicken with lemon
and tarragon 8, *9*
grilled chicken with lemon, garlic
and rosemary, served with
Puy lentils 12, *13*
grilled lemon chicken kebabs with
gremolata 48, *49*
Lentils
grilled chicken with lemon, garlic
and rosemary, served with
Puy lentils 12, *13*
Lime
stir-fried chicken with lime and
coconut *14*, 15

Mango
marinated chicken with honey and
ginger, served with mango and
sultana salsa *100*, 101
Maple barbecue sauce 70
Marinated chicken
marinated chicken brochettes with
green couscous 22, *23*
marinated chicken with honey and
ginger, served with mango and
sultana salsa *100*, 101
marinated chicken in a jar 26, *27*
marinated chicken satays with
peanut satay sauce 112, *113*
Marsala
chicken breasts with wild mushroom
and bacon stuffing and marsala
sauce 82, *83*
Mexican chicken chilli with yellow
tomato salsa *18*, 19
Moroccan baked chicken with chickpeas
and rice 116, *117*
Mushrooms
chicken breasts with wild mushroom
and bacon stuffing and Marsala
sauce 82, *83*
poached chicken breasts with
morel mushrooms, cream and
parsley 20, *21*
Mustard
herb-coated chicken with three
mustards 51
Nuts
crunchy pistachio-coated
drumsticks *88*, 89
oriental chicken stir-fry with broccoli
and cashew nuts 102, *103*
marinated chicken satays with
peanut satay sauce 112, *113*
Onions
chicken with roasted lemons,
red onion, thyme and garlic *74*, 75

apple, sage and onion
stuffing 124, *125*
Oriental chicken
oriental chicken *10*, 11
oriental chicken stir-fry with broccoli
and cashew nuts 102, *103*
Oven-baked chicken
oven-baked chicken with garlic and
Parmesan 61
oven-baked chicken in maple
barbecue sauce 70, *71*
Paprika
chicken paprika *28*, 29
Parsley
poached chicken breasts with
morel mushrooms, cream and
parsley 20, *21*
Parmesan
oven-baked chicken with garlic and
Parmesan 61
Pastry
chicken feuilletés 72, *73*
chicken and herb picnic pies 40, *41*
chicken and leek pot pie 120, *121*
Peanut satay sauce 112, *113*
Pies
chicken and herb
picnic pies 40, *41*
chicken and leek pot pie 120, *121*
Pistachio nuts
crunchy pistachio-coated
drumsticks *88*, 89
Poached chicken
poached chicken breasts with
morel mushrooms, cream and
parsley 20, *21*
Puttanesca 76, *77*
Rice
Moroccan baked chicken with
chickpeas and rice 116, *117*
Thai creamed coconut chicken
with Thai green rice 52, *53*

Roast chicken
fast-roast chicken with lemon
and tarragon 8, *9*
roast chicken with grape and herb
stuffing 58, *59*
chicken with roasted lemons,
red onion, thyme
and garlic *74*, 75
traditional roast chicken with
apple, sage and onion
stuffing 124, *125*
Rosemary
grilled chicken with lemon, garlic
and rosemary, served with Puy
lentils 12, *13*
Sage
apple, sage and onion
stuffing 124, *125*
cranberry, sage and balsamic
sauce 128, *129*
Salads
chicken salad with tarragon and
grapes 38, *39*
chicken Waldorf salad *92*, 93
curried chicken salad *54*, 55
Salsa
mango and sultana
salsa *100*, 101
yellow tomato salsa 18, *19*
Saltimbocca 90, *91*
Satay
marinated chicken
satays with peanut
satay sauce 112, *113*
Sauces
bread sauce 128, *129*
cranberry, sage and balsamic
sauce 128, *129*
lemon sauce 66
gravy *126*, 127
maple barbecue sauce 70
marsala sauce 82, *83*

peanut satay sauce 112, *113*
sherry vinegar and tarragon
sauce 64, *65*
stem ginger sauce 94
Sherry vinegar
chicken with sherry vinegar and
tarragon sauce 64, *65*
Spiced chicken 34, *35*
Spices, whole
chicken kebabs marinated with
whole spices and yoghurt, and fresh
coriander chutney 62, *63*
chicken with whole
spices *108*, 109
Stem ginger sauce 94
Stir-fried chicken
stir-fried chicken with lime and
coconut *14*, 15
oriental chicken stir-fry
with broccoli and
cashew nuts 102, *103*
Stuffings
apple, sage and onion
stuffing 124, *125*
grape and herb stuffing 58
wild mushroom and bacon
stuffing 82, *83*
Sultanas
marinated chicken with honey and
ginger, served with mango and
sultana salsa *100*, 101
Tarragon
chicken salad with tarragon and
grapes 38, *39*
chicken with sherry vinegar and
tarragon sauce 64, *65*
fast-roast chicken with lemon and
tarragon 8, *9*
Thai creamed coconut chicken
with Thai green rice 52, *53*
Thai green curry with
chicken 86, *87*

Thai red curry chicken 33
Thyme
chicken with roasted lemons,
red onion, thyme
and garlic *74*, 75
Tomatoes
chicken breasts with butter beans,
olive oil, chorizo and
tomatoes 30, *31*
Mexican chicken chilli with yellow
tomato salsa *18*, 19
Traditional bread sauce, 128, *129*
Traditional chicken giblet
gravy *126*, 127
Traditional roast chicken with apple,
sage and onion stuffing 124, *125*
Waldorf salad *92*, 93
Yoghurt
chicken kebabs marinated with
whole spices and yoghurt, and
fresh coriander chutney 62, *63*

Delia Smith is Britain's best-selling cookery author, whose books have sold over 16 million copies. Delia's other books include *How To Cook Books One, Two* and *Three*, her *Vegetarian Collection*, the *Complete Illustrated Cookery Course, One Is Fun*, the *Summer* and *Winter Collections* and *Christmas*. She has launched her own website. She is also a director of Norwich City Football Club, where she is in charge of Canary Catering, several restaurants and a regular series of food and wine workshops.

She is married to the writer and editor Michael Wynn Jones and they live in Suffolk.

For more information on Delia's restaurant, food and wine workshops and events, contact:
Delia's Canary Catering, Norwich City Football Club, Carrow Road, Norwich NR1 1JE; www.deliascanarycatering.co.uk
For Delia's Canary Catering (conferencing and events enquiries), telephone 01603 218704
For Delia's Restaurant and Bar (reservations), telephone 01603 218705

Visit Delia's website at www.deliaonline.com